Cambridge Elements ≡

Elements in Ancient Egypt in Context
edited by
Gianluca Miniaci
University of Pisa
Juan Carlos Moreno García
CNRS, Paris
Anna Stevens
University of Cambridge and Monash University

MAKING MEMORIES
IN ANCIENT EGYPT

Leire Olabarria
University of Birmingham

CAMBRIDGE
UNIVERSITY PRESS

CAMBRIDGE
UNIVERSITY PRESS

Shaftesbury Road, Cambridge CB2 8EA, United Kingdom

One Liberty Plaza, 20th Floor, New York, NY 10006, USA

477 Williamstown Road, Port Melbourne, VIC 3207, Australia

314–321, 3rd Floor, Plot 3, Splendor Forum, Jasola District Centre,
New Delhi – 110025, India

103 Penang Road, #05–06/07, Visioncrest Commercial, Singapore 238467

Cambridge University Press is part of Cambridge University Press & Assessment,
a department of the University of Cambridge.

We share the University's mission to contribute to society through the pursuit of
education, learning and research at the highest international levels of excellence.

www.cambridge.org
Information on this title: www.cambridge.org/9781009598552

DOI: 10.1017/9781009419017

First published 2025

A catalogue record for this publication is available from the British Library

ISBN 978-1-009-59855-2 Hardback
ISBN 978-1-009-41904-8 Paperback
ISSN 2516-4813 (online)
ISSN 2516-4805 (print)

Cambridge University Press & Assessment has no responsibility for the persistence
or accuracy of URLs for external or third-party internet websites referred to in this
publication and does not guarantee that any content on such websites is, or will
remain, accurate or appropriate.

Making Memories in Ancient Egypt

Elements in Ancient Egypt in Context

DOI: 10.1017/9781009419017
First published online: March 2025

Leire Olabarria
University of Birmingham

Author for correspondence: Leire Olabarria, L.Olabarria@bham.ac.uk

Abstract: Memory is a fascinating way to approach modern and ancient cultures, as it raises questions about what, why, and how individuals and groups remember. Egyptology has had a major impact on the development of memory studies, with Jan Assmann's notion of cultural memory becoming a widespread model within the humanities. Despite this outstanding contribution of Egyptology to memory studies, remarkably few recent works on ancient Egypt deal with memory from a theoretical and methodological point of view. This Element provides a general introduction to memory, followed by a discussion of the role of materiality and performativity in the process of remembering. A case study from Middle Kingdom Abydos illustrates how memory can be embodied in the monumental record of ancient Egypt. The purpose of this Element is to present an up-to-date introduction to memory studies in Egyptology and to invite the reader to rethink how and why memory matters.

This Element also has a video abstract: Cambridge.org/AECE_Olabarria_abstract

Keywords: memory, Middle Kingdom, stelae, Abydos, performativity

ISBNs: 9781009598552 (HB), 9781009419048 (PB), 9781009419017 (OC)
ISSNs: 2516-4813 (online), 2516-4805 (print)

Contents

1 Making Memories in Ancient Egypt

This year marks the centenary of the opening of the Hall of Memory in Birmingham in 1925. This building, located on Broad Street by Centenary Square (see Figure 1), was meant to provide a memorial for the over 12,000 citizens of Birmingham who died during the First World War. Nowadays it has become an imposing monument honouring those killed in other armed conflicts, with the website claiming that it remembers the people 'who gave their lives in the First World War, Second World War and in active service since 1945'.[1]

Farther along Broad Street, overlooking the canals of Brindleyplace, the Black Sabbath Bench stands proudly as a tribute to that local heavy metal band (see Figure 2). This steel bench was inaugurated on 26 June 2019, becoming a symbol of Birmingham and a memorial to the musical as well as industrial heritage of the city. While the Hall of Memory is conceptualised as a moving homage to senseless deaths, the Black Sabbath Bench presents itself as a playful reminder of the city's cultural ethos. In both cases, we see attempts to materialise memory through a conscious fostering of a shared public identity. These examples are a good illustration of some of the ways in which memory can work within individual and public consciousness. What this mobilisation of remembrance can achieve should not be taken for granted.

Memory is a fascinating way to approach modern and ancient cultures, as it raises questions about what, why, and how individuals and groups remember. Egyptology has had a major impact on the development of memory studies, with Jan Assmann's notion of cultural memory becoming a widespread model to understand the perpetuation of motifs, customs, and traditions over long periods of time. Despite this outstanding contribution of Egyptology to memory studies, remarkably few recent works on ancient Egypt deal with memory from a theoretical and methodological point of view. This Element provides a general introduction to memory, with a focus on aspects of materiality and performativity. The purpose of this Element is not only to present an up-to-date introduction to memory studies in Egyptology, but also to invite the reader to rethink how and why memory matters.

Section 2 provides some theoretical scaffolding to justify the approach adopted in the rest of the work. First, I present an overview of some of the main theoretical frameworks to the study of memory. From the pitfalls of strict definitions to the usefulness of broad categories, Section 2.1 outlines how disciplinary differences have affected understandings of memory over the years. A computational view of memory, where the human brain is perceived as a storage unit for information, has permeated both scholarship and popular perceptions of memory. Two well-known

---

[1] See website www.hallofmemory.co.uk/ (accessed 23 April 2024).

Figure 1 Hall of Memory (Birmingham, UK). Photo by the author

Figure 2 Black Sabbath Bench (Birmingham, UK). Photo by the author

approaches to memory, namely Jan Assmann's cultural memory model and Maurice Halbwachs' collective memory, are discussed in detail, paying particular attention to issues of communication and transmission. In this Element, I advocate for a more organic understanding of remembrance, where memories are constructed through lived experience and embodied action. Section 2.3 problematises a disciplinary divide between archaeological and textual research of memory in the study of ancient societies, favouring an integrated framework that sees inscriptions as an integral part of the materiality of objects.

A material approach to memory is the focus of Section 3. After a discussion of materiality, I take three main aspects to reflect on possible readings on memory from the material remains of ancient Egypt, namely monumentality, place-making, and performativity. In these sections, I explore how perspectives from theoretical archaeology and anthropology can be beneficial to help us reconsider a variety of Egyptian sources. In this context, I rely on the work on memory by Andrew Jones, and especially his concept of 'technologies of remembrance', which I take as a way to investigate how memory can be expressed by performative practice, to propose a model that rethinks how memories are constructed and perpetuated in the Middle Kingdom.

In Section 4, I introduce a detailed case study to showcase the potential of the model outlined in the previous section. I present the site of Abydos as a ritually charged location where memory played a crucial role. In particular, I focus on the so-called votive zone, where commemorative monuments, such as stelae, were erected in order to participate in a social culture of remembrance. I take three stelae belonging to a man called Nefernay, which have been identified as potential components of a votive chapel, namely ANOC 44, in the work of William Kelly Simpson. These stelae are studied as a meaningful group, exploring how they could have contributed to the communal construction of memory at the time by means of a deployment of elements of a rhetoric of commemoration. Some of the aspects that I focus on are their modes of transmission of ideas of hierarchy and status, their explicit interaction with other objects as well as with passers-by, and their contributions to the creation of a symbolic space of memory in this particular archaeological setting.

Finally, I provide a brief section, where I summarise some of the main conclusions of my analysis, and I reflect on the implications of perceiving Egypt as a culture of remembrance. Rather than focusing on the past in the past, here I turn the reader's attention to the past in the present. Memory continues to be reworked and actively constructed over time, so it makes sense to consider how Egypt is remembered in this context.

I first started thinking about memory in the framework of my research on kinship and monumental expressions of relatedness in Middle Kingdom Egypt.

By analysing the representation of social groups on the surface of commemorative stelae, I reached conclusions about the fluidity of conceptions of kinship in Egypt, which should not be seen as static and given, but as constructed and made over time. I was interested in how the visual registers of these stelae – both in terms of their iconography and their inscriptional material – had an impact on their audiences, potentially fostering and disseminating ideas about social groups. Thus, these stelae's functions were twofold: to commemorate those presented on them and to weave memories for others. This led me to conclude that a performative engagement with monuments was one of the bases of the practice of memory in Middle Kingdom Egypt, but I was left wondering how this operated in context and how we could reconstruct, if at all, the relational networks of meaning of which these stelae are an active part. This Element gives me the chance to reflect on these questions, exploring the rich possibilities that the material world of ancient Egypt has to offer.

2 Memory and Memory Studies

This section provides an overview of how memory is studied in different disciplines, with a focus on approaches from theoretical archaeology and sociocultural anthropology. Here I survey some recent publications about memory, assessing the impact they have had in Egyptological scholarship. I also examine to what extent these frameworks replicate certain disciplinary divisions between textual and archaeological understandings of memory.

2.1 The Impossible Task of Defining Memory

As part of a second-year module that I co-teach at the University of Birmingham, in October 2019 I had to deliver a lecture on letters to the dead. This textual genre comprises letters that were written by ancient Egyptians to their deceased relatives to appeal for help and assistance with a number of problems, ranging from issues with inheritance to requests of good health (for a recent overview, see Hsieh 2022). It was totally unplanned, but this lecture happened to be scheduled for Halloween, so I took the opportunity to chat to my students about the commemoration of the dead and how they were regarded as part of the social fabric at the time. We spent some time talking about what it meant to be an akh (ꜣḫ), identified as an active agent among the dead (see Troche 2021: 33–46), and often translated as 'ghost' in the scholarship. Just as I was telling them about a narrative text that has been dubbed an ancient Egyptian 'ghost story' due to the fact that it deals with one akh (see Section 3.1), the lights of the classroom suddenly went out, to the shrieking delight of my students. They kept reminding me of this spooky episode for the rest of the course.

Fast forward to the following year, the pandemic had struck. We were partially confined, and all classes were pre-recorded. I am sure I taught a lecture on the same topic in October 2020, but I have no recollection about it, and probably neither do my students. The setting where I recorded this lecture was exactly the same as for the other dozens of classes that I had to produce, and, talking to a blank screen, I could not feel a connection with those who were later going to watch it. I am sure many of the readers of this paragraph will have similar experiences, which highlight the importance of the setting to aid in remembrance as well as the delicate nature of memory, which is co-dependent with personal emotions. Despite the fact that we may all be able to recognise this subjective and personal nature of memory, we may struggle when prompted to provide a clear description of it, as memory is a multifaceted phenomenon, notably elusive to define.

One of the main problems affecting studies of memory is the notorious trap of analytical classification: there seem to be as many definitions of memory as there are authors working on it. Hallam and Hockey (2001: 3), for instance, note how memory can be understood 'as both the facility to remember and as the mental representation or trace of that which is remembered', bringing to the forefront a dichotomy between mental processes and actual recollections that poses a methodological challenge in scholarly approaches to memory. Indeed, such as distinction assumes that there is a categorical difference between the practice of memory and memories themselves; between recalling and what is recalled. Perhaps due to this methodological conundrum, vocabulary around memory can be paradoxically vague and precise at the same time. Terms such as 'memory', 'remembrance', and 'commemoration' are sometimes used almost interchangeably, but they can also be presented as strictly distinct categories with their own nuances by some authors. For example, Joyce (2003: 120) regards commemoration as a public marking of a shared social memory, and memory as the embodied experience of an iterative process. There is no agreement as to how these notions differ from each other, if at all; perhaps this is one of the reasons why Confino (2010: 79) has claimed that memory studies are 'more practised than theorised'. Be that as it may, definitions of memory and related concepts are dependent on the various interpretations of how memory works in practice.

Over the years, different (and often contrasting) models have been used to make sense of how memory operates,[2] with many of them being reliant on ideas of storage and information recall. Indeed, much of the work on memory since

---

[2] For an overview of approaches to the study of memory, see Foster (2009: 13–45). For a summary of philosophical aspects and understandings of memory, see Borić (2010: 5–16).

the Second World War has been based on computational models. These approaches understand the human brain as a powerful computer that codifies and retrieves information. Along similar lines, the 1960s saw the development of the 'multi-store' memory model by Atkinson and Shiffrin (1968). This framework postulates the existence of three separate 'systems', namely sensory memory, short-term memory, and long-term memory, with information being transferred between them in a sequential and linear manner. Other subdivisions of memory are also known in scholarship. For example, the distinction between episodic and semantic memory, initially postulated by Tulving (1972), illustrated an interpretation of two distinct systems of recalling stored information, the former based on personal experience and specific events, and the latter on more general culturally specific knowledge. The fiftieth anniversary of Tulving's chapter was marked by the publication of a special issue of the journal *Memory & Cognition* that appraised the contributions of this model to cognitive neurosciences (Brigard, Umanath, and Irish 2022). The reason why so many models postulate the existence of different systems or stages of memory may be that memory can be experienced as a 'multicomponent' phenomenon by the individual (Foster 2009: 39). While a subdivision of memory into different elements may be a useful way for us to categorise it, there is limited evidence that this is a fair and objective reflection of how memory works, and the separation of memory into phases or stages may not be as clear-cut as any of these models may suggest.

Something that we learn from these 'multicomponent' models is that there is a clear tendency to use metaphors to characterise memory (e.g., as a computer, as a repository, as a storehouse). These metaphors, however, do not explain how memory operates biologically. Instead, they illustrate how memory is understood socially, sometimes perpetuating those simplistic views of the human mind as a supercomputer that have been in vogue since at least the 1940s. Archaeologist Andrew Jones (2007: 5–12), whose work I explore in further detail in Section 3.3, presents a criticism of the limitations of the 'external symbolic storage' notion that interprets the mind as a container for a finite number of memories. Such models, he claims, consider the mind as an isolated entity and the external world as an objective and unquestionable reality. However, the human mind does not only process information, but it also creates it within a network of relations. This relational approach to memory is also favoured by anthropologist Tim Ingold (2000a: 138), who challenges this widespread understanding of memory as an 'inner cabinet' of the mind where information is stored. In an explanation of his 'dwelling perspective', which I return to in Section 2.2, Ingold (1993: 152–3) persuasively claims that 'remembering is not so much a matter of calling up an internal image, stored in the mind, as of engaging with an environment that is itself pregnant with the past'. If we accept this view, an alleged distinction between the practice of memory and memories themselves is not heuristically sound because memories emerge from the process of remembering.

What we also see here at play is a marked divide between empiricist and constructivist approaches to memory and the past. The former propose that there is a possibility to access the past 'as it really happened', so they understand the past as a concrete, specific, and bounded truth. The latter note that human memory does not reproduce the past as it happened, but (re-)constructs it on the basis of the impact that the world has on an individual. This may cause distortions of past events and feelings, which explains why memory is not a reproduction but a reinterpretation of the past. Different people may recall the same even in different ways, and that does not mean that any of them will be wrong, but that their experience has effectively shaped the different ways in which they remember the past. Thus, memory may be defined as a (subjective) reconstruction of the past in the present that does not exist in the abstract, but it is constructed and shaped through the act of remembering.

Given this vast array of definitions and classifications of memory, it comes as no surprise that many different methods have been used to interpret it, depending on the theoretical persuasions and interests of the researchers in question. In this sense, memory studies should in principle be treated as an interdisciplinary endeavour, where many theories and methods converge; however, when we explore publications on memory, it is obvious that there is a very clear disciplinary divide in existing approaches. For instance, Oxford University Press' *Memory: A Very Short Introduction* has been authored by neuropsychologist Jonathan K. Foster (2009), thus resulting in a work that is more oriented towards experimental and cognitive understandings of memory. When focusing on the uses of memory in the humanities and the social sciences, however, there are other aspects that have received more attention. For example, some scholars have been concerned with the impact of memory on the development of identity, while others have focused on the use of memory for the construction and manipulation of the past.[3]

References to the past are key when discussing the functions and uses of memory, and the fuzzy boundaries between history and memory are particularly relevant for our discussion. In the introduction to the *Companion to Cultural Memory Studies*, Astrid Erll (2010: 1–2) notes the difficulties inherent in any characterisation of memory, settling in a provisional definition as 'the interplay

---

[3] See Devlin (2007: 1–18) for a brief literature review of theories of memory in social sciences, particularly in archaeology and history.

of present and past in socio-cultural contexts'. Such a definition is, of course, not without its problems: it refers to an embedded interaction between past and present that has made many historians wary of the theoretical implications of memory as an analytical framework in terms of the impact it could have on the understanding of history itself. Indeed, studies of memory and uses of the past experienced a resurgence in the 1970s, when particular attention was being paid to practices of commemoration, especially in public settings. A renewed interest in political uses of memory and the past permeated a substantial number of publications around that time and beyond, to the point that it was understood by many as a paradigm shift within the humanities and the social sciences often referred to as the 'mnemonic turn'. Within this theoretical turn, memory is seen as a tool to assess the past, and a focus on memory as public discourse is identified as a way to challenge difficult political and historical legacies.

Sociologist Jeffrey Olick (2023: esp. 784–5) has recently reviewed and reconsidered the role of the mnemonic turn, analysing the epistemological background that led to an apparent reluctance of historians to embrace this 'new memory culture'. He notes that a recognition that memory is subjective, expressive, and particular could effectively challenge the primacy of history as a discipline. This potential threat to the reliability of historical approaches may have led to a judgemental attitude towards memory among historians, who have questioned the actual impact, scope, and robustness of the mnemonic turn. For example, Rosenfeld (2009: 151), whose work Olick critically appraises in his review, claims that memory studies are part of an intellectual trend that favours postmodern relativism, and which will 'decline in status with the intensifying desire for objective truth'. Rosenfeld and others claimed that memory studies was a fad that would soon disappear, and the implication here is that the disciplinary authority of history would then remain uncontested.[4]

Although the weight of the mnemonic turn has been questioned over the last few years, the following quotation provides a good summary of some recent scholarly engagement with memory studies, demonstrating they are as relevant as ever:

> By 2009, [. . .] there was not only the journal *History and Memory* (founded in 1987), but also the more broadly interdisciplinary *Memory Studies* (since 2008), along with a robust circuit of conferences, lectures, and workshops, special issues, books, edited volumes, book series, and even graduate seminars.

---

[4] Another example of this questioning of the disciplinary status of history as opposed to memory studies is given in Erll's (2010: 8) aforementioned introduction to her edited volume on cultural memory, where she explicitly states that history is simply a mode of cultural memory and historiography its main medium. Here history is seen as subordinate to memory studies, precisely the epistemological move that authors like Rosenfeld (2009) reject and fear.

Between 2000 and 2013, there was, according to a simple calculation based on Google Ngram, a 31-fold increase in book titles including the name (Maurice) Halbwachs. And while the major works of Aleida Assmann and Jan Assmann were not brought out in English until 2011 (though the English translation of Jan Assmann's *Moses the Egyptian* had appeared in 1997), their work was already having a profound impact in Europe, and the 1995 translation of Jan Assmann's essay 'Collective Memory and Cultural Identity' was a nearly instantaneous citation classic. In 2016, the Memory Studies Association was founded, and has since then grown to over a thousand members from more than 50 countries. Numerous individuals hold professorships with 'memory studies' in their titles, and there are now master's and other university programs in memory studies. (Olick 2023: 789–90)

Thus, it appears that memory studies, in one guise or another, are here to stay. Even if we conclude that its impact is not as profound so as to be considered a paradigmatic shift, memory is now embedded in the study of many disciplines in the social sciences and humanities, ranging from history to archaeology. Engagement with the past, either from the present or from the past itself, has become a well-established aspect of scholarship.

As I have shown in Section 2.1, memory can be many things, and this multiplicity of definitions means that memory resists being classified in any one-sided perspective, requiring a multidisciplinary approach. Scholars, however, have expressed concern over the fact that some studies of memory lump together phenomena that were previously studied separately, such as myth, tradition, biography, or national identity. For example, archaeologist Ruth Van Dyke (2019: 213–4) warns against the risk of conflating memory and culture, as that would lead to 'weakening memory's heuristic value'. Cultural historian Alon Confino (2010: 79) worries that the term is 'depreciated by surplus use'. Along similar lines, sociologist Vered Vinitzky-Seroussi (2001: 495) stated that '[i]f memory is everything and everything is memory, memory becomes such a catch-all phrase that it loses its significance'. It is true, as Olick (2023: 795) claims, that 'memory' can be problematic when utilised as a reifying category. I would argue that the flexibility and the ability to cross-fertilise the study of different areas is precisely what makes memory such a productive notion to explore, as it provides us with a window into the multifaceted nature of human experience. The lack of a unified understanding of memory should not deter us from using the term but rather encourage us to engage with it more meaningfully rather than taking it for granted.

In Section 2.2, I describe two of the most pervasive approaches to memory, namely social memory and cultural memory, reflecting on how they have helped shift the analytical paradigm in memory studies.

2.2 From Cultural to Social Memory

The topic of memory has garnered some attention in Egyptology over the last couple of decades. There have been works on commemorative practices at Deir el-Medina (Meskell 2003; republished as book chapter in Meskell 2004), studies of graffiti as creators of spaces of memory (Ragazzoli 2013), or, more recently, explorations of the topos of famine as a tool to mobilise social memory (Morris 2020, 2023). I would suggest that it is surprising, however, that not even more has been published, as what is arguably the most widespread modern theory of memory, namely the idea of cultural memory, was developed by the Egyptologist Jan Assmann. Cultural memory could be seen as one of the most extensive theoretical contributions of Egyptology to other disciplines, which is why I devote this section to explaining its scope and implications.

Jan Assmann developed his theories in the 1980s as part of a larger research project on the archaeology of literary communication (Archäologie der litera-rischen Kommunikation) established in 1978 at the University of Heidelberg. Indeed, Harth (2010: 88) describes the inception of the concept of cultural memory as a notion intricately linked to Heidelberg, where the Egyptological institute served as a 'centre of gravity' for the study of memory. At that institute, there was a policy of open association to facilitate interdisciplinary discussion through workshops, guest lectures, conferences, and joint research projects that encouraged rethinking and reshaping of ideas about memory. The project, initiated by Jan and Aleida Assmann, intended to map uses of cultural memory throughout history with a focus on the transmission of written knowledge, resulting in seminal volumes devoted to ancient (Assmann 2011b) as well as modern cultures up to postmodernism (Assmann 2011a). Jan Assmann was inspired by the work on social memory that had been previous advanced by, among others, Maurice Halbwachs. Halbwachs' model, which is often rendered as 'collective memory' in translations of his works,[5] refers to how remembering is mediated by the group and hence grounded in societies. I return to Halbwachs next, but first I explore the notion of cultural memory.

Jan Assmann (2011b: 5–7) differentiates four types of memory, namely mimetic, of things, communicative, and cultural. Mimetic memory is based on ritual actions, while memory of things focuses on the material dimension of individual recollections. On its part, communicative memory is a form of memory that is neither institutionalised nor formalised, and it can be perceived in everyday interactions. It focuses on people in relation to their recent past,

---

[5] Halbwachs' most widely cited work in English is *On Collective Memory*, which was published in 1992 as a translation of the work originally entitled *Les cadres sociaux de la mémoire* (compiled in a volume in 1952 posthumously after having originally appeared in a journal in 1925).

which Assmann (2010b: 111) understands as spanning around eighty years or three generations, so that it can be accessed by means of oral history. Communicative memory could potentially be understood as a reworking of Halbwachs' ideas due to this attention to lived memory, but Assmann (2010b: 109–11) stressed the distinction between the two notions: he regarded Halbwachs' approach as controversial due to an alleged binary separation of memory and history, and he criticised how Halbwachs downplays the crucial role of transmission. Be that as it may, the aspect that has shaped Assmann's theory more extensively is mainly cultural memory, which will be the focus of this section.

Cultural memory refers to the practice of activating the past in the present. It is a theoretical framework to explain how a number of fixed points in the past may become symbolic moments to which remembrance is anchored; this symbolic heritage plays a crucial role in the construction and perpetuation of collective identities. Those moments may be real or imagined, but what really matters is that they are used to construct a common past and to forge tradition through monuments and especially texts that embody those historical events, allowing states and their ideologies to persist over time. In a nutshell, Harth (2010: 92) proposes that 'cultural memory' should be understood as a hermeneutic category characterised by five features, namely (1) a differentiation of oral and literary processes of transmission; (2) an understanding of 'Kultur' as an authoritative, symbolically coded world of meaning;[6] (3) a definition of memory as a repertoire and generator of values; (4) the conventional use of sacralisation to standardise collectively accepted images; and (5) an organisation of script-based-culture as origin for active appropriation and continuation of those canonised traditions. While this focus on language and inscriptions may seem restrictive, it should be framed within the previously mentioned Heidelberg project on archaeology of literary communication, which was eminently text-driven.

The three core areas where cultural memory is meant to be more active, contributing to keeping the past in the present, are religion, art, and history (Assmann 2010a: 101). Hence, the notion of cultural memory has been adopted by Egyptologists to explain, for example, the perpetuation of motifs in art, such as the image of the king smiting his enemies, as argued by Luiselli (2011). However, Assmann (2011b: 20) notes that 'tradition' is simply an inadequate

---

[6] Harth (2010: 87) also makes an important point regarding the different semantic connotations of the term 'culture' in German and English, which is why he prefers to keep the German original 'kulturelles Gedächtnis' in his article. Culture (or 'Kultur') in the German tradition is a way to connect individuals to each other and to the world around them on the basis of shared norms (rules) and stories (memories). In the words of Erll (2010: 4), 'culture is a community's specific way of life.'

label for cultural memory, because it leaves out the fundamental aspect of reception. For him, cultural memory is concerned with reception and transmission, processes in which ideas are 'handed down' with a focus on the role of writing.[7] According to Assmann (2010b: 110–1), cultural memory can be 'exteriorised, objectified and stored away in symbolic forms that are stable and situation-transcendent'. In this way, cultural memory condenses all other aspects of memory, since a ritual, an object, and even language or communication can arguably be handed down as meaning. For instance, mimetic memory may well be expressed by ritual actions, but it is cultural memory that will assign meaning to those rituals, often through the actions of some 'special carriers' who could include 'shamans, bards, griots, priests, teachers, artists, scribes, scholars, mandarins, and others' (Assmann 2011b: 39). In this sense, active participation in the shaping of cultural memory can be perceived as highly differentiated, often in the hands of powerful elites in ancient times.

Assmann's theories of cultural memory have been very influential inside and outside Egyptology, contributing to a systematic understanding of memory and transmission of ideas. However, I would argue that there are three main methodological issues with this model. First, it is artificial to propose a clear-cut distinction between four types of memory.[8] Even if partitioning memory into discrete segments may seem useful from a heuristic point of view, as seen earlier, Assmann's division is unclear, as it suggests that meaning can be stripped away from actions and objects and considered independently. However, meaning does not exist in the abstract as an independent entity, but only within complex networks of relations. For example, it would be impossible to assign an absolute meaning to stelae and chapels from Middle Kingdom Egypt in an abstract sense without considering them as parts of a mosaic of relationships between people, objects, and landscape, as we will see in Section 4. Assmann's cultural memory provides an illustration of what Tim Ingold (2000a: 137–8) criticises as the 'genealogical model', which proposes a genealogical transmission of memory, rejecting environmentally situated experience as the core and focus of those memories. If memory is understood simply as acquired information available for transmission independent of its

---

[7] Aleida Assmann (2010a: 97–8) postulates that there is a difference between actively circulated memory (canon) and passively stored memory (archive), although she concedes that there is no clear distinction between what is to be circulated or stored.

[8] It is worth noting that Assmann's approach to memory is not always consistent throughout his publications, probably due to reworkings and reconsiderations of the validity of these categories over the years. For example, in one of his articles, Assmann (2010b: 109–10) advocates for the existence of three types of memory instead, namely individual, communicative, and cultural. An important point, however, is that communicative and cultural memories are always presented as distinct in his work.

contexts of application, then the environment and the mutual involvement in a number of activities will not play a role in the construction of such memories.[9] Instead, and following his 'dwelling perspective', Ingold (2000a: 146–8) highlights that knowledge and memory are situated and practised: memory and objects of memory do not pre-exist the act of remembering, but they mutually forge each other.

Second, there is the issue of agency on the transmission of cultural memory. Perhaps as a consequence of his interpretation of meaning as something that exists in the abstract, Assmann seems to argue for an almost direct transmission of ideas by means of members of the elite. While it is true that meaning can change and be adapted through time, Assmann's suggestion that 'special carriers' of culture would mediate and guide that process of transmission is debatable. Social inequality in relation to access to knowledge may have played an important part, as proposed by Baines (1990) in his study of restricted knowledge and hierarchy, but meaning cannot be imposed by external sources alone if it is understood to be enmeshed within complex networks of relations (see discussion on counter-memory in Section 2.3). Meaning is more difficult to manipulate, impose, and standardise than cultural memory suggests, and I continue to explore the idea of interdependence in the creation of memory in later sections.

A third problem with Assmann's notion of cultural memory concerns modes of transmission and reception. Assmann highlights the essential role of writing in the process of transmission and handing down of information. Cultures with no access to writing, Aleida Assmann (2010a: 105) argues, convey memory through performances and embodied practices and hence are limited in terms of what can be transmitted, but writing allows for an extension of horizons of knowledge. In other parts of his corpus, Jan Assmann elaborates on his understanding of the status of texts as carriers of meaning. For example, in *The Mind of Egypt*, Assmann (2002 [1996]: 6–11) presents an interpretative model that postulates a separation between material culture on one hand and texts or images on the other, noting that the former can be understood as objective whereas the latter are more 'semantically charged'.[10] In my view, on which I expand in Section 3, any model that separates material culture from textual remains is inherently flawed, but this framework explains the root of his focus

---

[9] Ingold (2000a: 148–50) has noted the dangers that this attitude poses for indigenous communities, whose knowledge and memories are informed and continually reforged in specific environments. Hence, removing those communities from their ancestral landscapes will make it impossible for their traditions, memories, and knowledge to be transmitted.

[10] The underlying thread of Assmann's argument in that book is a distinction between traces, messages, and memories, which maps onto alternative scholarly approaches in Egyptology, respectively archaeology, epigraphic/iconographic, and mythological.

on texts as carriers of meaning and perpetuators of memories. This is why authors like Harth (2010: 94) have defined culture (or 'Kultur', if one notes the special features of this term in German) as a 'dense fabric of writings'. In this model, memory is understood as something that can be handed down, preferably in writing, as if it were an heirloom; this promotes a very computational view of the human mind, shaped simply by inputs and outputs of information along the lines of the models advanced since the Second World War that I have introduced in Section 2.1.[11]

This straightforward transmission of units of memory may seem reminiscent of some problematic principles of evolutionary theory. The works of Richard Semon, a German biologist devoted to the study of memory in the late nineteenth and early twentieth centuries, postulate a parallelism between biological inheritance and the transmission of memory (Schacter 2001). His ideas find continuity in the notion of 'memetics', a model proposed by Richard Dawkins (1976: esp. 189–201) for the transmission of culture. Although Dawkins claims he developed his framework independently, both approaches are conceptually similar and demonstrate the uses of theories of genetics in the transmission of social knowledge. Memetics is an adaptation (pun intended) of Darwinian evolutionary theory to ideas of culture. Dawkins proposed an analogy between cultural and genetic transference that was based on the existence of a 'minimal unit of transmission'. In parallel to genes, which are seen as the smallest carriers of biological inheritance, Dawkins conceived of the existence of minimal units of culture that could be passed on from individual to individual, and for which he coined the term 'meme'.[12] An obvious problem with Dawkins' model is that it is difficult, if not impossible, to determine what a meme is and how the transmission process really works. Applying a biological template to culture downplays the complex ways in which culture and society inform each other. Dawkins' model is not acknowledged or cited by Assmann, but their ideas of transmission and 'handing down' of memory run in parallel, as they both speculate with the role of constructed minimal units of information to be transmitted.

As advanced earlier, I would argue that memory, like social knowledge and like culture, is created in and by relational assemblages that involve people, things, and environments. For that reason, rather than foregrounding an interpretation of memory that relies on modes of transmission, I am more interested in how memory works contextually. In this manner, I prefer to focus on the concept of memory as proposed by sociologist and philosopher Maurice

---

[11] See also Bernbeck et al.'s (2017: 15–8) criticism of Assmann's understanding of 'memory as a container' and 'memory as contained'.

[12] Cf. the notion 'mneme', proposed by Semon.

Halbwachs (1992 [1952/1941]). Halbwachs was inspired by his teacher and mentor Émile Durkheim to develop an understanding of memory that placed the process of remembering in the context of the group. This societal dimension of memory comes to the forefront of his work: for him individual memory exists, but only within the structure of a society (Halbwachs 1992 [1952/1941]: 53). This approach has been criticised because it has been considered to downplay the role of the individual (Gedi and Elam 1996), but instead I believe it shows how collective and individual memory are articulated and inform each other. For Halbwachs, individual memories are social phenomena, and people remember together because social groups provide anchoring points for their memories. He claims that '[w]hile the collective memory endures and draws strength from its base in a coherent body of people, it is individuals *as group members* who remember' (Halbwachs 1992 [1952/1941]: 22; my emphasis). To illustrate this point, in his introduction to the posthumous publication of Halbwachs' book (1992 [1952/1941]: 21), Coser explains how his experience as a migrant to the United States in the 1940s was made more difficult because he did not share a collective memory with his new colleagues.[13]

Despite having been developed in the first half of the twentieth century, Halbwachs' work was only rediscovered in the 1990s, perhaps as part of the mnemonic turn alluded to earlier.[14] Halbwachs' collective memory is placed at the level of the group, which is why I refer to it here essentially as a form of social memory. His notion has been criticised due to its 'inconcreteness' (e.g., Gedi and Elam 1996: 38), but, as we have seen earlier, flexibility and vagueness is an inherent characteristic of any definition of memory for it to be truly functional. I find Halbwachs' approach convincing because it is unified, treating memory holistically as a phenomenon mediated by society rather than artificially separating it into different categories. In his work, there may be many ways of remembering, but they are all conditioned by social experience, which, of course, includes other people, things, and the environment. For example, Halbwachs' (1992 [1952/1941]: 24) 'autobiographical memory' could be close to Assmann's communicative memory, but it is still explicitly anchored in the collective process of remembering. Groups, thus, will reconstruct their past and their memories together, which is an aspect I explore further next with reference to archaeology. In foregrounding the social dimension of memory, Halbwachs also acknowledges its relational character. Neither meaning nor memory exists

---

[13] See Olick (2023: 796–8) on how the use of 'collective' memory could potentially also be taken literally rather than seen as a metaphor.

[14] As shown by the essays collected on the seminal collective memory reader edited by Olick, Vinitzky-Seroussi, and Levy (2011).

in the abstract, so in order to understand commemoration, it needs to be inserted within the relational framework of which it is a constituent part.

Cultural memory and collective memory are two key frameworks to study remembrance. However, the limitations of the evidence available for ancient societies have shaped the ways in which they can be applied. In Section 2.3, I explore briefly how cultural memory and social memory have been used by different authors in their approaches to dynamics of memory in the past.

2.3 The Mnemonic Turn in Ancient Societies

In Section 2.2, I have introduced two of the most relevant and well-known approaches to memory in the humanities, namely collective memory and cultural memory, noting some of their advantages and disadvantages. They have both been keenly used by researchers working on memory in ancient societies, but they have had to be adapted to the types of sources available.

The mnemonic turn that I referred to earlier, namely the paradigmatic shift that sees memory as a way of assessing – and also confronting – the past, can also be recognised in studies of ancient cultures in two main ways. First, it is possible to identify a chronologically bounded explosion of publications on memory and material culture. While in the discipline of history, and more specifically in relation to the recent past, this resurgence took place towards the 1970s, memory studies penetrated the scholarship of ancient cultures around the turn of the century.[15] The archaeology of memory and remembrance, in particular, has received much attention over the last couple of decades, especially through collected volumes such as the ones edited by Williams (2003a), Van Dyke and Alcock (2003a), Barbiera, Choyke, and Rasson (2009) and Horn et al. (2020). Mortuary practices have been one of the prime locations for the study of memory in archaeology (Hallam and Hockey 2001; Devlin 2007), but the weight of memory is prevalent across archaeological studies.

A second way in which the effect of the mnemonic turn can be identified in the study of memory in societies of the ancient past is that memory is not only perceived as the past in the past, but also as the past in the present (e.g., Meskell 2007). Indeed, memory studies have been a political arena to denounce and challenge problematic pasts and traumatic events. As their counterparts working on the recent past, ancient historians and archaeologists have also engaged in a political use of their discipline in order to explicitly confront and shed light over events of the past that had been deliberately erased, such as legacies of slavery or the horrors of war. This practice of counter-memory as a way to

---

[15] It is noteworthy, however, that Egypt is conspicuously absent from many edited volumes on memory in the past (e.g., Dignas, Smith, and Price 2012; Dignas 2020).

uncover troubled and troubling pasts is understood by many as a moral responsibility. For example, Van Dyke (2019: 220) claims that to refuse to engage in archaeology as political action is an 'abnegation of responsibility'. This questioning of mainstream accounts and elite narratives through a reinterpretation of archaeology can also be spotted in the reassessment of the monumental record of the ancient past. For example, James Osborne (2017: 165–7) has written about the dynamic practice of counter-monumentality, the construction of and interaction with monuments with the specific intention to challenge memory by monumentalising a shameful episode of the past, inviting the viewer to critical reflection. This, he claims, was the role of Iron Age colossal statuary from Syria-Anatolia, whose post-installation treatment challenges traditional narratives that see these monuments as representations of royal power in the area. On a similar vein, in his study of remembering among the ancient Maya in Belize, David Mixter (2017) has theorised on how archaeology can provide a window to 'hidden transcripts' that are developed in resistance to official narratives often encountered in monumental discourse. The study of memory, then, reminds us of our responsibility to pursue a nuanced questioning of traditional narratives of the past, providing under-represented or historically undermined groups with an opportunity to have their voices heard. Thus, the historical accountability advocated by the mnemonic turn is also noticeable in the study of ancient cultures.

With these examples we also see how the study of memory in ancient cultures arguably reproduces some of the problematic disciplinary divides that I have identified earlier. In the case of ancient societies, academic disagreement is also presented in the form of the types of primary sources that different authors privilege. For example, some of the latest studies on memory in ancient Greece favour a textual approach to memory and transmission of ideas (Castagnoli and Ceccarelli 2019), with archaeological interpretations of memory being on the other side of this disciplinary divide (e.g., Alcock 2002; Hamilakis 2017). Much of the work on memory has unfortunately suffered from this ongoing siloing of disciplines, as well as from a misconception that assumes that literate societies will have access to a much larger repository of past knowledge – along the computational lines proposed by Assmann earlier – than those who rely on oral, performative, and embodied practices. As a result, the material dimension of memory has been overlooked in some treatments of memorial practices in ancient societies. There are many scholars, particularly prehistoric archaeologists, such as Richard Bradley (1998, 2002) or Andrew Jones (2007), who have demonstrated the potential of theoretical approaches to archaeology in the absence of written records, and some of their ideas can be productively applied to and adapted for historical contexts with writing. There are also many authors that remind us of the necessity of bringing these two approaches together, as inscriptions are an integral part of an artefact's materiality, as I argue in Section 3.

One of the reasons why scholars may have been tempted to privilege textual sources in their studies of memory in ancient societies is because texts may give us the impression that they reproduce ancient thought processes and emic conceptualisations more accurately. Whether texts provide windows to peer into ancient peoples' minds is debatable, not least because the purposes and features of the inscriptions determine the way in which ideas are presented. These sources should not be taken at face value to postulate how memory operates, but they are nevertheless sometimes used to (re)construct narratives of the past. However, we do not necessarily remember in a narrative, linear format (see comments on episodic memory earlier, for example), so it should not be assumed that a narrative is the only way in which to cast personal and collective recollections. This idea can be supported anthropologically. For example, when ethnographer Birgitt Röttger-Rössler (1993) attempted to collect personal memories for a study of social stratification during her fieldwork among the Makassar in Indonesia in the 1980s, she realised that it was not possible to ask individual members of the village to share their memories. Instead, the only way to extract this biographical information was to ask other villagers, who would naturally talk about other person's life in their presence, with the protagonist sometimes corroborating or adding to some details. This example of how the construction of (personal) memories is considered a social activity reminds us of how memory is not necessarily individual, but it can also be shaped by the community, along the lines postulated by Halbwachs. Such a collective construction of memory can also be attempted archaeologically. Indeed, the archaeological record never provides a 'complete narrative', but fragments and snapshots that we then need to weave together in our interpretations. In that sense, archaeological reconstruction of the past is comparable to reconstructions of personal and collective memory as modelled through inscriptions and needs to be inserted into a relational network that will be explored in further detail in Section 3.

Much of the research around memory in ancient Egypt has also relied mainly on interpretations of textual material, neglecting the role of material culture to some extent. While texts are an incredibly rich resource, a more complete picture will be attained by integrating inscriptions into their archaeological context. I would argue that one of the main reasons why the textual record has dominated studies of memory in Egyptology is not just due to the habitual focus on textual sources in this area study (Wendrich 2010), but, first and foremost, due to the influence of Assmann's work on cultural memory. As explained earlier, Assmann's approach is very reliant on written sources, and this model of memory, with its focus on written modes of transmission, has been adopted, adapted, and reproduced by many Egyptologists. Theoretical approaches to archaeology and material culture, however, have much to offer to Egyptology, and this is something that I explore in the following section, focusing on ideas of monumentality, performativity, and relationality.

2.4 A Material Approach to Social Memory

In this section I have explored different uses and approaches to memory. We have seen how the notion is extremely flexible, which could be seen both as a blessing and as a curse: on the one hand, it can be adapted to many different contexts, but, on the other, it risks losing some of its heuristic value. Memory is a flexible notion, and while this flexibility has been taken by some as a drawback, I am arguing that it makes nuanced explorations of people's relationship with their environment possible.

Different understandings of memory have been proposed, and in this section I have focused on social and cultural approaches to memory, providing overviews of the seminal work of Jan Assmann and Maurice Halbwachs. I have also argued that perhaps an excessive reliance on Assmann's model of cultural memory has caused Egyptology to focus primarily on texts and, as a result, to disregard the potential of other sources of evidence, falling behind in the development and application of theoretical frameworks of memory that are taken from archaeology, particularly those pertaining to embodied, performative, and relational approaches.

Definitions of memory may seem quite abstract, but in order to access memory archaeologically one needs to assume that its traces can be materialised to some extent. This means that memory should not be understood as an exclusively mental practice, and the material expressions of remembrance deserve further attention. In the following section, I explore the material dimension of memory, and particularly the concepts of monumentality, place-making, and performativity, and their relationship with remembrance.

3 The Materiality of Remembering: Monuments, Places, and Technologies of Remembrance

As argued in the previous section, scholars are far from offering a single and unified definition of memory in the past. On the one hand, different cultures may have conceptualised and enacted memory in various ways, rendering universal definitions inadequate. On the other, and depending on the theoretical persuasions of the authors, either textual or material sources have been presented as an optimal avenue to assess memory. This distinction disregards that texts are also essentially material culture and that inscriptions participate in the materiality of the objects that bear them. For that reason, this section focuses on materiality and its role in the study of memory in the past. In particular, I discuss how monumentality plays a crucial role in the presentation and dissemination of cultural ideas, and I use the notion of 'technologies of remembrance' in order to assess specific ways in which a monument may mobilise remembrance. I also briefly explore the link between materiality and forgetting by considering the effects and consequences of the destruction of monuments.

In a recent article, Ruth Van Dyke (2019: 209) has stated that 'archaeology is memory all the way down', because it focuses on the 'construction of social memory as deployed and created through engagement with material things and places'. This approach invites us to reflect not only on what those material things and places really are, but also on how those engagements can be traced in the archaeological record. Although one may argue that a distinction between things and places is irrelevant, as both mutually inform each other, I will keep that heuristic separation for the purposes of this section, where I first explore how materiality interacts with memory, particularly through monuments, and then move on to consider how those artefacts of memory create meaning in particular locations and through specific embodied actions.

3.1 Material Things: Monumentality and Memory

The relationship between materiality and remembering is important for archaeological research, as noted in the previous section. Memory can be manifest in rituals that have material expressions and that may be, in some cases, archaeologically retrievable; for example, votive objects could crystallise a process of commemoration. In this way, it makes sense that we could study memory in connection with materiality.

Materiality itself is, like memory, a difficult concept to define (Miller 2005: 4; see also Harris and Cipolla 2017: 89–94). As a starting point, we could say that materiality is a theoretical framework that highlights the qualities of a material, what things *really* are in a tangible way: the flexibility of polymers, the ductility of metal, the porosity of wood, or, as Timothy Taylor (2009: 381) puts it in his introduction to materiality in a handbook on archaeological theory, the 'essential thingness of things'. This approach reflects common definitions and expectations about what 'materials' are, but it also presupposes that there should be a 'thingness' in things and that material qualities can be studied independently of meaning and use. There is a similar intellectual challenge, as noted by archaeologist Julian Thomas (2007), inherent in the concept of 'material culture', which seems to imply that culture that is *not* material could also exist.[16] However, 'culture' cannot simply exist in the minds of individuals independently of the material world around it.

These discussions are pertinent to current developments in Egyptological scholarship as well. For example, there is a trend to incorporate the notion of materiality as a theoretical framework in the study of ancient Egypt. The popularity of recent research projects on the 'materiality of writing' is an example of this current scholarly turn. Essentially, these approaches try to focus on the 'material' and 'tangible' aspects of writing (e.g., composition of the ink, thickness of the ductus, strokes of the pen) that have been traditionally disregarded in many studies of Egyptian texts. In that sense, these projects provide a unique and timely opportunity to redress some of the past focus on abstract philological approaches. However, the use of 'materiality of writing' as a phrase also assumes that writing could be stripped off its materiality, which is not the case. The 'text' does not exist independently from its 'manuscript' and speaking of a 'materiality of writing' could invite us to perpetuate dualisms that do not necessarily exist ontologically. Rather than relying on dualistic distinctions, my approach to materiality recognises the interconnectedness and mutual informing of objects and humans, who exist and interact within assemblages of relationships.

One of the scholars who has reflected on the meaning and implications of materiality for Egyptology from a more nuanced theoretical perspective is Lynn Meskell. In her book *Object Worlds in Ancient Egypt*, Meskell (2004: 7) concedes that 'Egyptian culture placed enormous emphasis upon material rendering and representation as an instantiation of individual permanence, cultural longevity and the endurance of powerful socio-religious concepts'. This is a key aspect of any approach to memory and 'permanence' in Egypt, which can be seen to be mediated and represented by means of material traces such as monuments. Egypt is indeed often regarded as a culture of monumentality, where many buildings and artefacts were created in order to leave a material trace. This sense of permanence of stone architecture is what Jan Assmann (1988, 1991) has referred to as 'stone time'. In a recent discussion on monumentality in Egypt, Richard Bussmann (2019: 101–2) notes how monuments are linked to memory in general and to cultural memory as an elite practice specifically.[17] Indeed, the impact of the monumental discourse on the

---

[16] On discussions around material culture, see Boivin (2008), Meskell (2004), and Knappett (2005). For an intellectual history of the 'material cultural turn', see Hicks (2010).

[17] Interestingly, he goes on to remark how a cultural memory of Egypt based on monumental discourse runs the risk of forgetting the social contexts where those monuments are created and gain their meanings. This argumentation is in line with the discussions on counter-monumentality and 'hidden scripts' introduced in Section 2.3.

memory of groups of the past should not be underestimated. For example, David
Petts (2003: 194–5) studied how stone memorials in the early Middle Ages not
only helped to recall memories but also reproduced and recreated social knowledge. Thus, the monumental discourse can be said to sustain social practices,
and it contributes to a meaningful construction of the present and a legitimation
of the past. The problem here, as usual, is to gain some unified understanding of
what a monument is.

There are indeed many definitions of monument in scholarship, from those
that try to quantify monumentality on the basis of expenditure and labour (e.g.,
Levenson 2019: 28–9; Buccellati 2019: 42–7; Brysbaert 2018) to those that rely
on more qualitative ideas of symbolic power (e.g., Osborne 2014: 9–13). Some
authors have even tried to come up with a checklist of features that would allow
to classify something as monumental; for example, Brunke et al. (2016: 255)
propose that monumentality should be determined on the basis of size, position,
permanence, investment, and complexity. On their part, Alvarez and Grebnev
(2022: 2) have noted the fluidity of the term 'monumental', which may convey
grandiosity in a variety of ways. Although they concede that size or grandeur
have traditionally been regarded as key characteristics of monumentality, the
social experience must also play a fundamental role. In this sense, physical
environment, cognitive impact, and social lives of monuments become all
marks of their essence.

Monuments provide a valuable example of this link between materiality and
memory. Monuments are generally made to endure, and many of them may
feature inscriptions pointing explicitly at a desire for commemoration. The
Oxford English Dictionary defines monument as 'a statue, building, or other
structure erected to commemorate a famous or notable person or event // or in
memory of the dead', so the idea of commemoration seems to be inherent in
shared understandings of what a monument is. This is hardly surprising, as the
etymology of the term goes back to the Latin *monere*, 'to remind, to warn, to
advise'. In a collection of essays on memory and forgetting in postmodernity,
cultural critic Andreas Huyssen (1995: 26) even referred to the study of memory
as 'a cultural obsession of monumental proportions'. This statement, perhaps
tongue in cheek, places emphasis on the undeniable link that exists between
monumentality and memory. A monument, then, is some kind of landmark
whose main purpose is intrinsically linked to commemoration.

An association between monuments and remembrance also existed in ancient
Egypt, and it can be traced unequivocally in ancient inscriptions. The term mnw
('monument') is related to the verb mn ('to endure, to last'). A Middle Kingdom
stela of Montuhotep, for example, reads as follows: 'my name shall be good and
lasting [mnw] in (my) city, and my monument [mnw] shall not perish forever'

(London UC 14333; Landgráfová 2011: 260–3). Monumentality and permanence are presented as intrinsically connected in this inscription, where the expectation is that the 'name', that is to say, the reputation and standing of an individual, should be perpetuated through the enduring permanence of this object.

Some of the formulae that point at the importance of having one's name remembered employ the term sḫꜣ, which could also be used both for monument and for memory. The verb sḫꜣ ('to remember') is indeed used in several stock phrases, such as variations of the relatively common formula 'it is my good name that you should remember', which reiterates the importance of having one's name perpetuated, in parallel to the expression presented in the previous paragraph. Shubert (2007: 364) suggests that this phrase may be associated with the rites of Osiris because viewers can be asked to remember the name of the deceased at particular festivals of this god, with some attestations of these formulae associated with Abydos chapels, which I discuss in Section 4. For example, the stela of Dedu (see Figure 3) shows a clear association with a ritual landscape, probably the one of Abydos: 'it is my good name that you shall remember [sḫꜣ] at the temple of Osiris' (Durham Oriental Museum EG503 [N.1932]; Simpson 1974: pl. 48 [ANOC 31.1]). These and other inscriptions present the site as a stage for memorialisation, with the festivals of Osiris and the proximity to his temple regarded as potent complements to the perpetuation of memory.

The content and purpose of this 'good name' formula is similar to that of the so-called vivification formula (dỉꜥf rn꜀f sꜥnḫ, 'may he cause his name to live'), which is attested from the First Intermediate Period onwards, becoming ubiquitous in the later Middle Kingdom (Nelson-Hurst 2010: 13). The most recent and extensive treatment of the related formula sꜥnḫ rn ('to make one's name live') postulates that it played a key role within a memorial ritual in ancient Egypt (Rizzo 2024). An explicit example of how this formula would work is the stela of Intef (British Museum EA 562; Simpson 1974: pl. 12 [ANOC 5.3]), where the first two lines of the inscription read: 'may the officials who will pass by speak, may they give me effectiveness [ꜣḫ] that I may live from the breath that people give, that they may make my name live'. This inscription links the very existence of the monument with the ability of the stela owner to be remembered, as the carving of his name on the surface of the monument will prompt passers-by to pronounce it and hence make it live again. Here the inscriptions emphasise a performative and interactive side of remembrance that I revisit and expand upon next.

In this sense, and from a terminological point of view, it can be argued that a connection between memory and monumentality remains true from an emic ancient Egyptian lexical perspective. Memory is seen to have a material

Figure 3 Stela of Dedu. Durham Oriental Museum EG503, ANOC 31.1.
Reproduced with permission from Oriental Museum, Durham University

dimension that will make commemoration possible. By virtue of being a culture
of monumentality, Egypt can also be considered a culture of remembrance.

Alvarez and Grebnev (2022: 4) also note how inscriptions, sometimes disregarded as secondary insertions into objects, are in fact an integral part of
monumentality. Inscribing monuments grants them an additional semiotic and
communicative dimension, and it may also be a way to reinforce memorialisation, as seen in the previous example of the perpetuation of the name of a stela
owner. Remembrance is actively enacted, for instance, through so-called
appeals to the living, which are inscriptions where a deceased individual entices

passers-by to utter their name (Shubert 2007; Yamamoto 2015). In Section 4, I explore the implications of appeals to the living for the study of memory as an embodied practice through a case study, but suffice to say here that passers-by were often addressed with a promise of a mutually beneficial arrangement. The Middle Kingdom stela of Montuhotep (Cairo CG 20539; Lange and Schäfer 1902a: 150–8; 1902b: pls xli–xlii) highlights that compromise of reciprocity, as the act of remembrance is seen to provide benefits to both parties involved: 'as for the one who will remember [sḫꜣ] my good name, I shall be his protector by the side of the great god, lord of sky, in the presence of the great god, lord of Abydos'. The concept of ma'at is relevant in this context. Assmann (2002 [1996]: 127–34) understands ma'at as 'connective justice', highlighting the importance of reciprocity in the Egyptian cosmovision. He notes that commemorative practices provide an opportunity for social reciprocity, which translates into social cohesion. Commemorating others upholds ma'at and ensures the maintenance of the social fabric according to tradition.

Such reciprocity and interaction were not only expressed in terms of facilitating remembrance, but also explicitly as a way to avoid forgetting. For instance, after an appeal to the living that asks visitors to perform an invocation offering for the butler Ipi, it is noted that 'you will cause that I be remembered [sḫꜣ] without my being forgotten [smḫt]' (Liverpool World Museum M.13846; Gardiner and Sethe 1928: pl. xi). Here forgetting is seen as an undesirable alternative to remembrance, which is activated and enacted through interaction with the living.

A variety of written sources reinforce this connection between monumentality and memory by highlighting the risk of being forgotten when monuments are destroyed or damaged. For example, the early Middle Kingdom inscription of Intef (see Figure 4) reads, 'I found the ka-chapel of the noble Nekhty-iker, being destroyed, (its) walls being old and all its statues being broken, and there was no one who would remember [sḫꜣ] it' (Berlin Inv. 13272; Landgráfová 2011: 32–4; Lange 1896). This implies that something can only be remembered when it leaves a physical, monumental trace. At the bottom of the same stela, Intef also refers to the reason why he may have rebuilt the ka-chapel of Nekhty: 'I did all this so that my name may be good on earth and so that the memory [sḫꜣ] of me may be good in the necropolis.' In this part of the inscription, Intef concedes that restoring this monument may provide some reciprocal benefits, as he himself will also be remembered for that deed.

Inscriptions claiming to have restored monuments are well known. For example, De Meyer (2005) studies nine inscriptions left by Djenutinakht, son of Teti, in tombs of Dayr al-Barsha and Shaykh Said, possibly in the late First Intermediate Period. In these texts, he claims to have restored the tombs of his

Figure 4 Stela of Intef. Berlin Ägyptisches Museum Inv. 13272
(after Lange 1896: pl. ii)

ancestors by 'making firm that which was found destroyed, renewing that which was found in ruin' (De Meyer 2005: 126). There is no clear indication that Djenutinakht restored tombs belonging to his direct predecessors; instead, these almost identical texts targeted the most extensively decorated tombs of these two cemeteries. This leads De Meyer (2005: 132–3) to suggest that the reasons for restoring these monuments are less altruistic than these inscriptions imply, probably linked to legitimation and personal gain. Being remembered together with those powerful individuals, and hence accruing status through this material connection, would have been one of the main outcomes of this practice.

It is unclear to us from these inscriptions whether any damage to these monuments was intentional or simply due to the passage of time, but this question opens up interesting avenues of research regarding deliberate erasure as retribution or punishment (Connor 2018). Preservation of monuments was a clear concern for the ancient Egyptians (Di Teodoro 2022), and keeping them in a good state was seen as a necessity for those monuments to be fully functional. In the case of tombs, for example, that would entail having their funerary cult established, and, hence, their memory perpetuated. The so-called ghost story that I referred to in Section 2.1 gives us a unique glimpse into these ideas. In this New Kingdom text, which has been reconstructed from several fragmentary sources (Beckerath 1992; translation by Wente in Simpson 2003: 112–5), a priest called Khonsuemhab encounters an akh that is causing trouble in the Theban necropolis. The reason for this is that his tomb was in very poor condition. He mentions how he had been buried in a well-equipped tomb with a large shaft, which had fallen into disrepair: 'see, the ground beneath had [deteriorated] and dropped away. The wind blows (there) and [seizes a tongue]'. In order to appease him, Khonsuemhab promises to 'prepare the tomb anew' for him, re-establishing the endowment for his cult offerings with daily libations and deliveries of grain. Overall, this literary text draws attention to the crucial role of monuments in the maintenance of memory and avoidance of forgetting.

Although many of these inscriptions seem to focus on individual remembrance and this could suggest that group remembrance was secondary, the presence of multiple figures displayed on the surface of stelae – or indeed represented across other monuments that could have been grouped together archaeologically (Olabarria 2020b: 49–50) – shows that groups were also part of that practice of monumental remembrance. Members of the kin group and other colleagues were mentioned on stelae, completing and enhancing the self-presentation of the individual. Stela Durham EG502 (previously N.1942; see Figure 5) provides an interesting example of group remembrance, as the stela owner, Djefy, invokes '(Those whom) I have known, (those whom) I have not known, (those whom) I have remembered [sḫꜣ], (those whom) I have forgotten [smḫ]. (My) female workers and male workers, every man of the hꜣw, the pr of the father and the pr of the mother, my friends, all my people' (Olabarria 2018: 65–6). By including everyone he remembers and forgets, Djefy presents himself as someone with a large entourage, which ultimately reinforces the power of memory: when people are remembered, they remain present and thus continue to exist. This stela is being analysed here in isolation because its archaeological context is not known, but it is worth thinking about whether its location (e.g., close to other stelae or in connection with other chapels where some of these people were mentioned or displayed) could have complemented the message that was being communicated.

Monuments, as bearers and enactors of memory, play a crucial role in the process of remembering, but they cannot be said to create memory on their own; instead, they act within those networks of relations from which memory emerges. The idea of monumentality itself may need to be reconsidered and nuanced under this interpretative light. If the focus is placed on interactions and relations, the difference between what is and what is not a monument may be blurred. For instance, Ingold (1993: 169; 2000b: 175–81) challenges the idea of a clear-cut distinction between built and non-built environments because the buildings themselves are not given, but rather eventually emerge from people's interaction with the landscape. As he puts it, a feature may be more or less a building in different periods, so the 'buildingness' of a space is relative. This may be reminiscent of my questioning of the 'thingness of things' at the beginning of this section. Along the same lines, the 'monumentality' of a monument is also something that should not be taken for granted. This is

Figure 5 Stela of Djefy. Durham Oriental Museum EG502. Reproduced with permission from Oriental Museum, Durham University

one of the many problematic aspects of fixed classifications, which is why we should focus on what a monument does rather than on what a monument is.

Overall, a connection between memory and monumentality is evident from ancient Egyptian sources from the Middle Kingdom and beyond. The enactment of memory was understood to be intrinsically linked to and prompted by material culture. Monuments attract the attention of an audience who will 'make live' the name of those displayed on them. Thus, inscriptions tend to highlight a reciprocity that is inherent in any act of commemoration. Along the same lines, a link between destruction of monuments – whether intentional or not – and forgetting is noted. This focus on materiality, however, raises questions around processes of remembrance. Who are they enacted by? Where do they happen? What impact do they have on their agents? In Section 3.2, I explore how remembrance can be anchored to specific spaces that contribute to the emergence of memories.

3.2 Places of Memory: Anchoring Remembrance

In the introduction to their volume *Archaeologies of Memory*, Van Dyke and Alcock (2003b: 2) note that memory can be explored through ritual behaviours, narratives, representations and objects, and also places. The addition of 'places' to this list is indicative of a situated perspective that recognises that material culture can be anchored in specific locations that contribute to shaping and perpetuating those memories. According to geographer Tim Cresswell (2015: 22–3; following Agnew 1987), a place can be defined as a 'meaningful location'. I adopt this approach here, as it provides an encompassing framework that merges ideas of built and natural environments, landscape, and meaning. In this context, memory is integral to any holistic understanding of place, as it will contribute to imbuing it with meaning.

Cresswell (2015: 25–6), however, goes on to suggest that the difference between 'place' and 'landscape' is that landscape is observed from the outside, while a place is something to be inside of, a distinction that I do not endorse here, as it assumes that a landscape is an external, static, and objective unit. In my view, one should not conceive landscapes as passive and immutable products of anthropic action, but as agents that inform human behaviour in profound and meaningful ways. Ingold (1993: 163), with his notion of 'taskscape', has placed emphasis on how landscapes emerge relationally through networks of activities and interactions between objects, people, and the landscape itself. As such, a taskscape is perpetually in process, and I follow this lead here by placing the focus on relationality.

Memory, again, is essential to understanding the meaning of any location. Following Ingold (1993: 152–3), perceiving and experiencing a landscape ultimately constitutes an act of remembrance in itself, because that landscape has been constructed and reshaped by actions of previous and current generations. Monumental spaces, as well as landscapes, have been studied from an experiential perspective through the effect they have on their audiences. Joyce (2003: 111) claims that monuments are 'ambiguous', since they are exceptionally visible while potentially encapsulating invisible spaces, thus triggering access to different levels of memories. In my opinion, this purported ambivalence is not problematic, but rather a core feature of monuments, which exist on several different levels and may mean different things to different people over time. Joyce's idea of monumental ambiguity may stem from a visual bias; indeed, ideas of location and visibility have deeply influenced discussions of monumentality and experience of the landscape (Ma 2007: 209–13). Many recent archaeological discussions on landscape have centred on the undeniably crucial role of visibility (Buccellati 2019: 52–3; Jiménez-Higueras 2020; Sullivan 2020). However, as some of these authors also acknowledge, monuments are not only visible, but also audible, tactile and, in sum, rendered perceptible by an array of sensory experiences (Parkinson 2020). For example, the cheering of the crowd during a procession, or the physical touch of the desert sand, could contribute to the experience of a monument and to the construction of its multiple layers of meanings.

This focus on experiential and sensory aspects of landscape has provided insightful avenues of research. Van Dyke and Alcock (2003b: 5–6), in the same introduction cited earlier, argue that 'place is a sensual experience' because it articulates human perception through presence and inhabitation. In this sense, it is interesting to explore the role of experiential and phenomenological approaches to the study of memory. This phenomenological turn can be traced back to Heidegger and his 'dwelling' perspective, which assumes that humans cannot be separated from the world they inhabit (Harris and Cipolla 2017: 96–7). In a clear rejection of dualistic analytical frameworks, there is no 'interior mental' world separated from an 'exterior material' world, but a total interdependence between people and objects.

Such a phenomenological approach has clear implications for the study of landscape and monuments, as illustrated by the work of Christopher Tilley (1994), clearly inspired by Heideggerian perspectives. He observed how many works in archaeology simply present sites as 2D maps in their publications. This means that most archaeologists' understanding of different sites would be mediated through a bird's-eye view. As a response to this prevalence of 2D renderings, he started visiting a number of sites, walking along ancient routes, noting down anything he saw and felt, such as the effect of the sunset or the experience of mounds around him. This focus on sensory aspects allowed him to propose a different understanding of Neolithic landscapes. Whereas this approach may seem speculative, Tilley's intention was not to try and reconstruct any given ancient experience, but to show that there are – and were – a variety of forms of experiencing the landscape, and that they all could have an effect on constructions of meanings around it. A critical aspect of this phenomenological turn in the study of landscape and memory is the notion of embodiment, which I explore in further detail in Section 3.3.

As Tilley (1994: 25) points out, landscapes acquire sedimented layers of meaning through the events that take place in them, but a sensory engagement with the landscape can be further mediated by emotions. Traumatic events have been considered powerful conductors to the cementation of memory at a particular place. For instance, the location of an accident or a terrorist attack may become particularly moving for those directly affected but will also have an impact on the collective memory of the community (e.g., Truc 2011). In the same vein, anthropologists and archaeologists have studied concentration camps as powerful centres of memory (e.g., Myers 2008). The experience of a place, however, does not need to be traumatic in order to inspire feelings and create meaningful emotional links. For example, Halbwachs (1992 [1952/1941]: 193–235) studies places of pilgrimage as sites of memory, noting the impact of collective practices on the anchoring of memory to specific places. Tombs are seen as having special relevance in studies of how memory is created, perhaps because of that emotional component that may be attached to the performance of memory by and for the dead. For instance, grave assemblages have been assumed to encourage particular ways of remembering in different societies (Hallam and Hockey 2001; Williams 2003b: 16). Cemeteries and votive sites in Egypt could also be regarded as emotionally charged places where memory may be particularly potent and active, as shown by the emphasis on remembrance in inscriptions illustrated by examples in Section 3.1. Landgráfová (2011: xxi–xxii) used the term 'memoscape' to denote these places that are laden with individual and social memory, but it is worth highlighting that a place does not display or embody memory on its own.

Philosopher Pierre Nora (1989) coined the term 'lieux de mémoire' (i.e., 'places of memory') to refer to places where collective memory is crystallised from a material, symbolic, and functional perspective. He developed this concept specifically to study aspects of French nationalism, and he was interested in the reciprocal interaction between memory and history. Since its introduction, the notion of 'places of memory' has been adopted as an analytical category somehow uncritically by many researchers. The term, as proposed by Nora, is more focused on historical implications of commemoration and their use in the construction of a shared past than on the effect memory and landscape have on each other. As I have argued so far, memory is not *stored* in objects or places; it is relationally performed, so a suggestion that a place can encapsulate and accumulate a nation's memories on its own and be able to transmit specific ideas about national identity should be seen with caution.

The spatial dimension of memory, however, is fundamental to understanding those relational networks involving people, monuments, and memory. For example, social groups may reuse or rebuild monuments to reaffirm and reinterpret claims to space, which may have been further emphasised through performance and commemorative ceremonies. These successive reappropriations of the landscape are what Patricia McAnany (1995) calls a 'genealogy of place' in relation to the Maya context, where successive burials of people of the same family facilitated a claim to a land through those ancestors. In her own words, 'places with long chains of transmission will also have long sequences of construction events punctuated by dedicatory and commemorative cache deposits as well as actual ancestor interments' (McAnany 1995: 104–5). Such a perspective, as noted by Roman archaeologist Darrell Rohl (2015: 10), 'shifts the frame of reference from the past to the present', recognising all those layers of meaning are in a constant process of construction, hence allowing for deep narrative approaches. As opposed to Nora's conception of 'place of memory', which sees civic and national identity as almost fossilised in some key landmarks, genealogies of place recognise the dynamic and continuous reworking of the nature of memories associated with a location, placing particular emphasis on the assemblages from which those memories emerge.

The notion of genealogy of place can be productively applied to societies where monumental memorialisation is used to display a sense of belonging through the construction of actual or symbolic space. For example, David Petts (2003: 25) describes the grave as a testimony to a claim made over the land by particular social groups in early medieval Wales. An ethnographic parallel is posed by Maurice Bloch's (1971: 108–24) thought-provoking discussion of how monuments, particularly tombs, are used in the construction of social groups and their symbolic claim over the land among the Merina of Madagascar. In ancient Egypt, memorial chapels at Abydos also were inserted into a physical landscape that was claimed by display, sometimes with successive additions to that ritual landscape (see Section 4). In these genealogies of place, memory is constructed through space, as monuments create and sustain ideas of society within developing conventions of funerary and votive display.

In Section 3.1, I have noted how some inscriptions could help locate acts of commemoration. In the stela of Dedu, discussed earlier (see Figure 3), we read how the stela owner requests for his name to be remembered specifically at the temple of Osiris, arguably in Abydos. Here remembrance seems to be locational, as the inscription transforms that temple into a stage for memorialisation. What we see in this example is an anchoring of memory to a site, but this should not be perceived as static, as the physical link of monuments with the place they were intended for is not guaranteed. The extent to which an architectural landmark is permanently and physically fixed in the landscape can be questioned: tombs and temples from ancient Egypt have been transported out of their original location. The Old Kingdom tomb chapel of Hetepemakhti, currently in

Leiden, is an example (Mohr 1943), and some architectural features, such as obelisks, statuary or even construction bricks, are also known to have been moved in antiquity (Osorio G. Silva 2023). Even though their location may have changed, and this adds further layers of meaning to their biographies, it does not preclude the significance of the original location for which they were created. In his study of early medieval Welsh burial sites, Petts (2003: 193) argues that stelae that are moved from their original location may continue to act as reminders of the deceased in whose memory they were created, as well as of the social and physical landscape for which they were intended. Portable objects, such as votive offerings, are equally reminiscent of an archaeological context. As I will explore in Section 4, Abydene stelae are an excellent example of relatively portable objects linked to a particular space, as their essence can only be understood in light of the role they played in the celebration of the festivals of Osiris, namely the desire of people to participate in them through their monuments. It is for this reason that I would argue that 'place' can also be symbolically created. This approach to experiences of the past through the landscape will be revisited in Section 4, where I focus on the site of Abydos.

3.3 Engagements: Embodied Remembrance and Performativity

In Section 3.1, I have shown that monumental inscriptions reveal some of the specific methods that groups of the Middle Kingdom carried out to achieve that perpetuation of memory. These included repeating a person's name, restoring and maintaining their monuments, and also linking their remembrance to a physical or symbolic place. Those strategies employed by social actors of the time to encourage remembrance on an audience can potentially be traced in the monumental record of ancient Egypt in the Middle Kingdom in a variety of ways.

In the edited volume *Archaeologies of Remembrance: Death and Memory in Past Societies*, archaeologist Andrew Jones (2003) published a chapter entitled 'Technologies of Remembrance: Memory, Materiality and Identity in Early Bronze Age Scotland'. In this work, he introduced what he called 'technologies of remembrance' to refer to processes of materialisation of memory in Bronze Age Scotland. These technologies embody regularities and commonalities that are achieved by means of repetition, pointing at the crucial performative aspect of these practices. An example he gives is cremation, which he sees, in the case of Beaker burials in northeast Scotland, as seeking to activate remembrance without the need of a monumental landmark (Jones 2003: 82).

The notion of 'technologies of remembrance' was later expanded in his monograph *Memory and Material Culture* (Jones 2007). Jones here proposes that artefacts should be interpreted neither as units of information nor simply as symbols, but instead as mnemonic tools that have an impact on the audience. In this context, he highlights how memory does not exist in the abstract; instead, he focuses on the networks of relations and on how they themselves elicit memory. In his own words (Jones 2007: 26), 'memory is not a function of the internal processes of the human mind, but memory is produced through the encounter between people and the material world'. Thus, he claims that interactions between funerary artefacts, places, and performativity can create and recreate memory of the deceased (Jones 2007: esp. 41–5). What this means is that remembering, as I have been arguing in this Element so far, is not something that simply happens, but something that is done. In this process, we can recognise a kind of double agency: those who are commemorated use some socially sanctioned methods that resonate with those who commemorate them. In the next section, I apply this idea of 'technologies of remembrance' to a case study from Middle Kingdom Abydos, with a focus on display and performativity, but I first want to explore further the issue of embodiment in terms of how engagements with the material world come to be.

Given my earlier discussion on memory and monumentality in Middle Kingdom Egypt, we could assume that display is a key method to ensure remembrance, as allowing others to see a monument would be essential for it to have an effect on the audience. This is specifically mentioned in the inscription of Intef from Berlin explored in Section 3.1 (see Figure 4), which implies that, if a monument is ruined, there would be no one who would remember the person to whom it was dedicated. Egyptians used different techniques to attract attention to their monuments in this context of competitive display; this could be through sheer size (e.g., Olabarria forthcoming) or exceptional design elements, such as perforated openwork ankh-signs (Hill 2010) or mummiform figures (Whelan 2016). However, following Jones, just having a monument is not enough, no matter how memorable its display elements may be; interaction with an audience, with the environment, and with other monuments would be required for the emergence of remembrance. Indeed, the notion of technologies of remembrance reminds us that objects do not represent memory on their own, but they are focal points in an assemblage of relations and social practices that includes material culture, landscape, as well as people and their physical actions and material engagements.

The importance of physical actions for the enactment of memory was highlighted by anthropologist Paul Connerton (1989), whose notion of embodied commemorative performance has been well received by archaeological theorists (e.g., Meskell 2007: 224). Connerton (1989: 4–5) argues that the process of remembering is facilitated by bodily practice: 'if there is such a thing as social memory, I shall argue, we are likely to find it in commemorative ceremonies; but commemorative ceremonies prove to be commemorative only in so far as they are performative; performativity cannot be thought without a notion of bodily automatisms'. As we see from this quotation, Connerton's idea of memory is anchored in iterative performance and embodied experience.[18] This is a quasi-phenomenological approach that challenges computational models of memory, associating memory with personal experience and perception instead. Connerton's embodied commemoration highlights ideas of performative practice around objects, practices that can also contribute to giving cohesion to a group along the lines of 'technologies of remembrance' postulated by Jones.

Connerton (1989: 72–3) draws a distinction between two practices to illustrate how memory is 'sedimented'. The first one is an 'incorporating practice', which refers to activities that need the presence of the body for a message to be transmitted. The second one, an 'inscribing practice', concedes that there may be ways to record information for transmission when the body is not present or has stopped informing. He also notes (1989: 75) that the transition from an oral to a literary culture is essentially a transition from incorporating to inscribing practices. This separation has been questioned by some archaeologists (e.g., Hamilakis 2013: esp. 89; Van Dyke 2019), who, of course, recognise that the process of inscribing should equally be seen as a bodily practice. Connerton (1989: 76), however, is aware of this and even devotes a section of his book chapter to characterise the 'irreducible bodily component of writing'. His motivation for proposing a separation of incorporating and inscribing practices is not to question the bodily dimension of such inscribing practices, but to reflect on what they do and how they function as a mnemonic system. In that sense, and derived from Connerton's terminology, it may be possible to argue for an inscribed incorporation of these actions. He claims (1989: 102) that inscribed sources have been privileged in the study of memory, but that bodily action is likely to be more resilient to discursive criticism because it exists through performativity, and it is formalised through automatisms. In Connerton's framework, bodily memories will actually – and in opposition to Assmann's model of cultural memory presented in Section 2.2 – be more effectively sedimented than inscribed ones, because they have become unconscious and unintentional. Van Dyke (2009: 222–3) is particularly concerned by the adequacy of the concept of intentionality in this context. According to her, discursive memory is often

---

[18] Assmann (2006: 70–2) has also written on bodily automatisms, ritualised action, and their relation to memory in Jewish and Christian tradition. However, he differentiates between a primary, functional level of action, and a secondary, symbolic one, in line with his understanding of memory as a hermeneutical practice.

presented as an intentional practice in opposition to practical memory, which is seen as a habitual, automated, and hence unintentional action, but discursive practices can also have unintended consequences and reworkings, so their intentionality can also be questioned.[19]

Despite these criticisms, Connerton's focus on bodily practice is stimulating and thought-provoking, but we are still left with the question of how to find traces of those actions in ancient societies. Some of those incorporated practices that emerge as a result of iterative performance may be inferred from technologies of remembrance, and these could have been materialised and perpetuated in the monumental record.[20] Bodily practice and performativity are, hence, a way to establish a link with other mnemonic communities that share a similar culture of commemoration.

Ancient inscriptions can indeed be used in order to access and eventually decode some of those gestures and actions that may be presented as a token for incorporated memories. For example, some of the monumental inscriptions seen earlier describe how the utterance of the name was desired in order to enact commemoration. In those cases, we can see an emphasis on reciprocity, but also on bodily performativity, through repeated utterances and through other embodied actions. For example, the stela of Wahysobek (see Figure 6) features an inscription that reads: 'O those who still live on earth, any scribe, and any person who shall pass by this stela of mine. As you desire that your local gods should favour you, so should you say the breath of life to the nose of Wahysobek, living again' (Cairo CG 20164; Lange and Schäfer 1902a: 195–6; Lange and Schäfer 1902b: pl. xiv). Here we see clearly how a person who is being commemorated is actively requesting a specific action from the audience, namely to get close to the figure of Wahysobek represented on the stela, to pronounce that vivification formula to his nose and activate that remembrance.

It would be fair to speak here, following Valerie Hope (2000: 186), of a 'rhetoric of language' that mobilises remembrance. We need to remember, however, that many people who saw these stelae may not have been literate (Baines and Eyre 2007). In some cases, there may have existed partial literacy, especially given the visual quality of hieroglyph script, where some signs could have been recognised and act as a trigger for some ritual actions (Zinn 2018). Moreover, some of those inscriptions could have been read aloud so people who may not have been able to read them directly may still have had access to the messages they were conveying.

---

[19] For a brief discussion on intentionality with reference to Gell's material agency, see Olabarria (2020b: 14–23).

[20] See also Hamilakis (2013) for a focus on multi-sensoriality and bodily memory.

Figure 6 Stela of Wahysobek. Egyptian Museum, Cairo CG 20164 (after Lange
and Schäfer 1902b: pl. xiv)

In addition, it is worth pointing out that inscriptions did not exist in
isolation, being often interwoven with iconic representations. As such, as
well as a rhetoric of language, we are faced with a 'rhetoric of images'
(Hope 2000: 186), where certain gestures and actions performed by figures
on comparable stelae may have been widely recognised as gestures that

would elicit practices of remembrance. The Middle Kingdom stela of Seneb (Vienna ÄS 156; Oppenheim et al. 2015: 197) features a number of figures in a gesture of declamation that could invite those passers-by who could not read to perform comparable actions, pronouncing an invocation offering for the dedicatee of this monument (see Figure 7). These are examples of how memory does not simply happen, but it needs to be enacted through performative, embodied action. In Section 4, I explore these devices of visual rhetoric with reference to one case study featuring multiple stelae.

Overall, a performative conception of memory, which can be actualised by means of bodily actions and iterative practices, provides a model that involves individuals, groups, objects, and landscapes. Remembering is thus something that one does, not just something that happens by itself, and it should be understood within this relational network.

3.4 Remembering through Materiality

In this section I have explored the material dimension of memory, arguing that materiality is only one of the aspects in the intricate relational network from which memory emerges. Here I rely primarily on Halbwachs' conception of memory as a phenomenon mediated by society to situate remembering in the context of the group, and to argue that memory is actively constructed and performed.

Monuments may have contributed to the creation of spaces of memory, but they did not enact memory on their own. Andrew Jones' notion of 'technologies of remembrance' invites us to think of the possible ways in which commemoration could be prompted through iterative practice. Among those strategies, monumental display is fundamental, being recognised in ancient inscriptions as a key to remembrance. However, we have seen how explicit interactions with those monuments were also required in order to keep memory alive and active. Such interactions illustrate the importance of performative action that could be elicited in inscriptions through a rhetoric of language and/or in iconographic representations through a rhetoric of images. Some of those performative aspects of memorial practices may also give cohesion to a group and contribute to the creation of dynamic places of memory where layers of meaning are accumulated over time.

In the next section, I present a case study from Middle Kingdom Abydos in order to illustrate how this materiality of remembering can be identified and analysed in practice.

Figure 7 Stela of Seneb. Vienna Kunsthistorisches Museum ÄS 156
(© KHM-Museumsverband)

4 Middle Kingdom Abydos as a Place of Memory

In the previous section, I have discussed how memory does not exist in the abstract, but it emerges from a network of relations that includes objects, people, landscapes, and all their interactions. I also noted how there are ways in which those relations may be brought to the forefront in the enactment of memory through so-called 'technologies of remembrance'. These need to be assessed within specific contexts, as expressions of localised understandings of memory embodied in social interactions. We now turn to a case study in order to demonstrate how these technologies of remembrance are constructed and actualised in a specific context, namely the site of Abydos in the Middle Kingdom.

4.1 Abydos as a Site of Memory

Abydos is a unique case study to assess how embedded memory is in the landscape and in its monuments, because it was a sacred site used over hundreds of years (see Figure 8). However, it is worth pointing out that there are many other sites in Egypt where memory plays a pivotal role. For example, Hana Navrátilová (2020: 149) has utilised so-called visitors' graffiti to propose an interpretation of Memphis and neighbouring regions in the New Kingdom as spaces of and for social memory, where inscribing the landscape conflates ritual and memorial practices to interact with the past. The sanctuary of Heqaib in Elephantine provides a prime example to investigate how a local community would interact with their ancestors by means of votive offerings and dedicatory practices in the Middle Kingdom (Jiménez-Serrano 2023).[21] Saqqara also stands out as a site where commemoration is apparent in the monumental record, and Lara Weiss (2022: 9–10) proposes the use of 'reminiscence clusters' as a category of analysis to understand who was commemorated and what strategies were used. While Abydos is not the only site that could have been chosen for this exercise, it is a potent and meaningful example of mnemonic construction in Egypt. As authors such as Janet Richards (1999), Ute and Andreas Effland (2010, 2013) or Matthew Adams (2019) have shown, Abydos boasts layers of topographical, political, mythical, and historical meaning, all of which give coherence to the site as a ceremonial centre as well as a conceptual landscape.

Abydos, located in southern Egypt, was saturated with cultic importance since predynastic times. The region known as Umm el-Qa'ab, where the German Archaeological Institute has been undertaking excavations since

---

[21] For a comparison of Abydos and Elephantine as sites of votive practice, see Olabarria (2020b: 126–9).

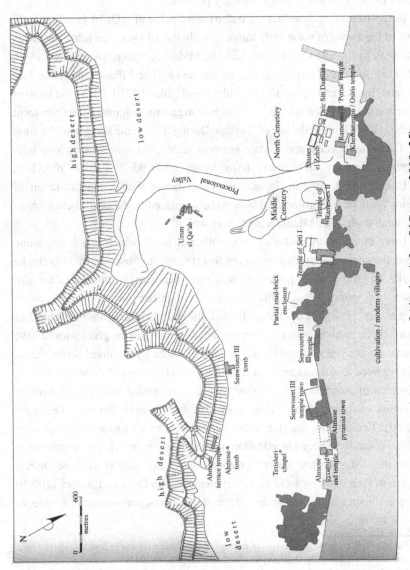

Figure 8 Monuments of Abydos (after O'Connor 2009: 25)

1978, is particularly relevant to this discussion (Dreyer 2007).[22] Some of the earliest archaeological remains at the site include high-elite tombs, such as the well-known tomb U-j, which bears witness to the oldest attestation of early Egyptian script (Dreyer 1998; Regulski 2014). These remains show the relevance of this area already in these early periods.

Rulers of the first dynasties were also buried at Umm el Qa'ab (see Figure 9). One of the tombs of these early kings, namely that of Djer, was reinterpreted as the tomb of the god Osiris himself in the Middle Kingdom (Amélineau 1899: 91–115). As part of a research project directed by Ute Effland since 2006 (see Effland, Budka, and Effland 2010; Effland and Effland 2010, 2013), the tomb of Djer has been re-excavated in order to investigate the origins and development of the cult of Osiris at the site of Abydos. During the Middle Kingdom, the tomb of Djer was opened and a staircase was added, showing interactions with previous funerary architecture (Amélineau 1899: 95–7; Petrie 1901: 8–9; O'Connor 2009: 89–90). In addition, a sculpture with a representation of Osiris lying on a mortuary bed was probably placed in the central chamber of the tomb during the Middle Kingdom as well.[23]

Umm el-Qa'ab translates as 'the mother of pots', which is a fitting name given the amount of pottery recovered from the site: as observed by Julia Budka (2019: 85), millions of pottery vessels were deposited in honour of the god Osiris in a period of over 3,000 years as part of celebrations known in scholarship as the 'Mysteries of Osiris'. Indeed, the wadi leading from the Temple of Osiris to the tomb that was reinterpreted as belonging to the god seems to have been used as a processional route, becoming an area for ritualised performance, as suggested in sources such as the stelae of Ikhernofret.[24] Along that route, hundreds of commemorative stelae were erected on the sides of the wadi by devotees who wanted to participate in those festivities in honour of Osiris for eternity. Those stelae, together with other monuments such as statues or offering tables, could have been placed within mudbrick memorial chapels commemorating the dedicatee and his or her entourage in the context of these Osirian feasts. In their work on archaeology of memory, Van Dyke and Alcock (2003b) note that memory can be studied through narratives, representations, objects,

---

[22] For summary of the project and list of publications, including regular excavation reports, www .dainst.org/projekt/-/project-display/63453 (accessed 15 April 2024).

[23] For a description of the bed and its discovery, see Amélineau (1899: 109–15; pl. iii). Effland and Effland (2013: 17–20) have been able to reconstruct the location of this Osiris bed within a newly discovered limestone shrine.

[24] The text on this stela refers to the celebration and performance of a procession representing the triumph of Osiris over his enemies. See also Cahail (2022: 130–7) for a reconstruction of the rituals described in Ikhernofret's inscription in relation to a large seasonal inundation lake that would form on the floodplain north of the Temple of Osiris.

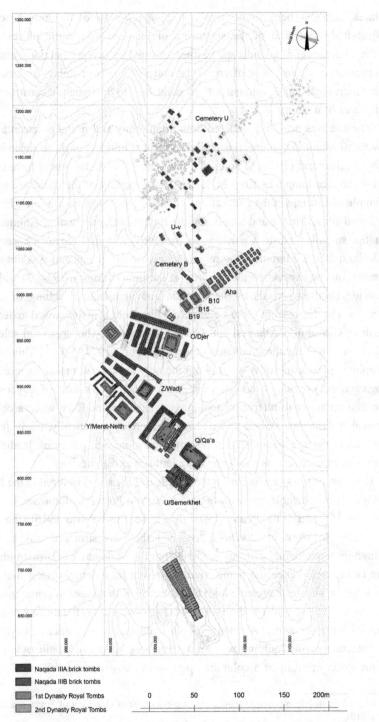

Figure 9 Plan of Umm el-Qa'ab (© DAIK, drawing by Martin Sählhof)

places, and also behaviours. This is a good reminder of the importance of contextualisation and of the anchoring of memory to specific places. The cultural meaning of a landscape has been shaped by layers of actions, and the deposition of those votive offerings, be pottery vessels or stelae, demonstrate how individual and communal actions contribute to the dynamic constructions of places of memory.

The site was heavily plundered both in antiquity and in the nineteenth and twentieth centuries, so the archaeological context of many of those stelae is not known. Simpson (1974: 8) notes that the majority of stelae would have come from the area known as Kom es Sultan, in the vicinity of the enclosure of the Temple of Osiris, via the excavations conducted by Auguste Mariette, French colonial administrator and founder of the Egyptian Department of Antiquities, in the so-called North Cemetery in the early and mid-nineteenth century (Guilhou 2021). Mariette, who relied heavily on his agents and was not even present during excavation the majority of the time (Simpson 1974: 2), did not provide detailed records of the location and architectural setting of these objects. The dispersal of these stelae across the world is mainly owed to dealers such as Giovanni d'Athanasi and Giovanni Anastasi, who organised sales in 1837 and 1857 for these coveted objects (Simpson 1974: 5–6).[25] This indiscriminate plundering of Abydos is not the only aspect that makes its archaeological history extremely complicated. The long and deep history of Abydos has made it attractive to many archaeologists over the years. Even when archaeological excavations started to be recorded more systematically, many teams worked at the site with different research questions and priorities, leading to a mosaic of excavations having been undertaken at the site.[26]

One part of the site adjacent to the temple of Osiris was covered in the New Kingdom by a temple that excavators called 'the Portal of Ramesses II' (see Figures 10a and 10b). Petrie (1903: 7, 18; see also Petrie 1916), the first excavator to work in this area, assumed that this structure was a New Kingdom monumental gateway leading from the enclosure of Osiris to one of the cemeteries, hence the name 'portal'. It was later demonstrated that this structure was instead a temple built by Ramesses II in an area of prime importance due to its proximity to the Temple of Osiris, which was the starting point of the Osirian procession at Abydos and a place of sacred significance in itself. The architecture of the building was quite damaged, but a brick-built pylon and some lower sections of a columned portico in stone were visible (O'Connor

---

[25] On unregulated excavations at Abydos and the dispersals of object out of Egypt, see Taylor (2019).

[26] Summaries of the history of excavations at Abydos can be found in, for example, Richards (2005: 125–56), Yamamoto (2009: 10–21) and Snape (2019).

(a)

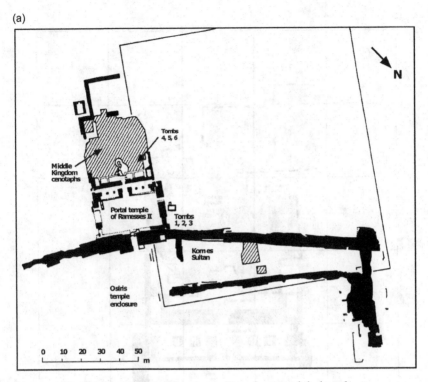

Figure 10a Portal of Ramesses II and memorial chapel area
(after Simpson 1995: 2)

1967; see also O'Connor 2009: 117–9). The temple also featured Osiride statuary and colossal figures of Ramesses in recessed niches. This area was excavated in 1967–1969 by a joint team from the University of Pennsylvania and Yale (O'Connor 2009: 93), uncovering a significant number of mudbrick chapels arranged in close proximity to each other. The construction of the temple of Ramesses II had razed many monuments almost to the ground,[27] but it also led to the preservation of the foundations of those chapels underneath the floor levels of the temple (O'Connor 1985; Silverman 1989). This area is known as the 'Terrace of the Great God', and it offers a prime example of how commemoration is enacted through public (and competitive) display. This votive area is the focus of Section 4.2.

---

[27] Ramesses II was not the first ruler to destroy earlier monuments at Abydos. Following mainly ceramological evidence, Yamamoto (2009) argues that some structures housing stelae would have been demolished around the time of Senusret I in order to facilitate the constructions of a plastered pavement close to the Temple of Osiris. Abydos was indeed a dynamic ritual landscape.

(b)

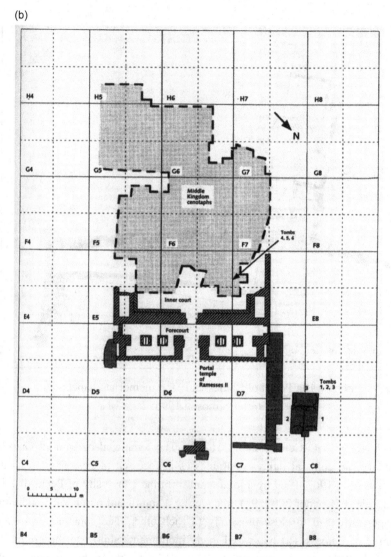

Figure 10b Portal of Ramesses II and memorial chapel area
(after Simpson 1995: 3)

4.2 The Terrace of the Great God

The area often referred to in Egyptological scholarship as the 'votive zone' was
a focus of ritual activity in the Middle Kingdom, as demonstrated by the many
inscriptions referring to the 'Terrace of the Great God',[28] from where devotees

---

[28] On the identification of the 'Terrace of the Great God' with the votive area at Abydos, see
Olabarria (2020a: 126–7).

would participate symbolically in the festivities in honour of the god Osiris taking place at the site. As mentioned earlier, this zone was filled with mudbrick buildings, which have been interpreted as votive chapels.

The plans published by the Pennsylvania-Yale team give us a glimpse of what this area of Abydos would have looked like (see Figure 11). The plans show an

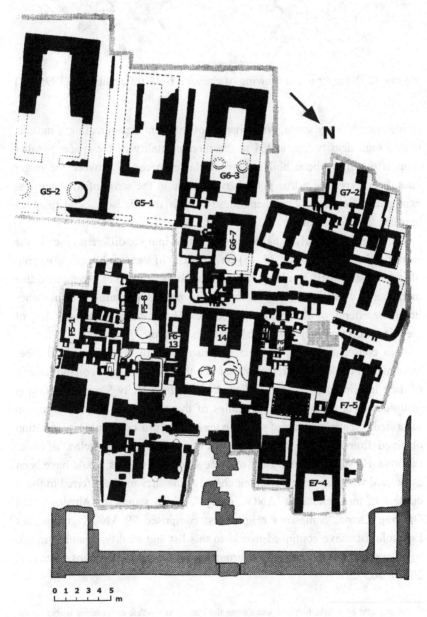

Figure 11 Plan of memorial chapel area (after Simpson 1995: 32)

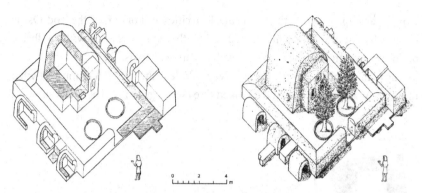

Figure 12 Reconstruction drawing of chapel F 6–14 (after Simpson 1995: 32)

architecturally busy space, with chapels of different sizes creating a mosaic, with a high density that added to the monumentality of the space. Smaller chapels may have been built in any available spaces in between the larger ones, hence creating a true genealogy of place in the sense of McAnany, as explored in Section 3.2: perhaps these chapels materialised social relations between the dedicatees.

The chapels themselves have been classified into six different types in the work of Yamamoto (2009: 35–45) on the basis of their architectural morphology. These chapels would all have housed stelae and other commemorative monuments, either inside a small vaulted chamber (see Figure 12) or in niches lining the exterior of a solid core of mudbrick. However, the complex history of the site means that very few have been found in situ.[29]

As a consequence, the potential reconstruction of how stelae (and other monuments) could have been clustered into those chapels relies on the reading of their inscriptions. The seminal work of William Kelly Simpson (1974) is instrumental in modern understandings of these Abydene chapels. Simpson identified potential clusters of stelae on the basis of prosopographic information obtained from personal names and titles inscribed on the stelae, often as captions. He suggested that each of those groups of objects would have been associated with a specific mudbrick chapel at the site, and he referred to those clusters of monuments as 'ANOC groups', which stands for Abydos North Offering Chapel. Simpson's original list comprised 79 ANOC groups, but Egyptologists have continued to add to this list and modify existing groups, so the current list of known ANOC groups stands at about 110 groups (Olabarria 2020b: 205–22).

---

[29] An example of a stela found in situ during the Pennsylvania-Yale excavations is that on the forecourt of chapel E-7 (Simpson 1995: pl. 6b).

What these ANOC groups remind us of is that Egyptians may not have seen individual stelae as units of commemoration. Instead, perhaps it was those clusters of monuments, in their materialisation of those social connections, that one should turn to in order to reconstruct uses of social memory at the site. It is worth exploring whether those chapels may have been conceived as places of memory in the sense presented in the previous section.

Inscriptions on stelae reveal that Egyptians themselves did understand them as parts of larger assemblages, with chapels being identified as discrete units. For example, the stela of Minhotep (British Museum EA 202; Simpson 1974: pl. 3 [ANOC 1.6]; Olabarria forthcoming) includes a column running down the centre of its surface that explicitly states that a chapel would be comprised of stelae: 'it was (my) father Ikhernofret who commanded that this stela is set up for (me) in his chapel [mꜥḥꜥt] of vindication'.[30] By setting up a stela in someone else's chapel, social connections are being created and fostered through such monumental practices.

Although there is some uncertainty around who visited Abydos as part of religious feasts during the Middle Kingdom,[31] the votive zone provides a unique opportunity to reconstruct how an audience would interact with monuments in a way that would facilitate remembrance. John Baines (2006: 290) points out, with reference to large-scale festivals, that much of their symbolic incorporation must have been exclusionary. Indeed, some parts of the festival were kept secret, and we have only an approximate reconstruction of the performances and rituals that took place during the Middle Kingdom, mainly through the stela of Ikhernofret (e.g., Olabarria forthcoming; Cahail 2022). However, participation seems to have been a main feature of the festivals that took place at Abydos. If visiting some of these chapels was an activity to be undertaken during local festivals, then the community feeling among participants may have been reinforced.

There are in fact some ways in which engagement with these monuments could initially seem to be restricted, such as in terms of the location, size, or accessibility, but further analysis shows that symbolic access to these places of memory was a priority. Space was at a premium in Abydos, as confirmed by later inscriptions such as the stela of Neferhotep (Leahy 1989), which started to regulate the use of the area from the 13th dynasty onwards.[32] This lack of space contributed to the high monumental density of the site, which may have made

---

[30] On the translation of mꜥḥꜥt as chapel, see Olabarria (2020a: 128–32).

[31] On Osirian festivals at Abydos, see also Kucharek (2006), Smith (2017: 226–36), and Végh (2019, 2021).

[32] See also Whelan (2016: 310–15), who claims that the popularity of solid core chapels may be due to this lack of space.

the area difficult to navigate. Looking at the Pennsylvania-Yale map in Figure 11, it seems that all mudbrick chapels could be reached through some kind of path or processional road. Their location within the site would perhaps determine whether some of the chapels would have been easier to reach than others, something that could have played an important role in this context of competitive display.[33]

Access to stelae would have also been determined by the architecture of the chapel where they were housed as well. Yamamoto (2009) and Kopleff (2017), for example, have demonstrated how the dimensions of chapels at the site were not uniform. Some of the chapels would have been quite low, so stelae installed inside would only have been visible when crouching or squatting. This means that one would have had to actively seek them, either because of a personal connection or because it was part of the expected experience of pilgrimage to Abydos. In addition, O'Connor (1985: 102) highlights that some chapels in the votive zone featured a courtyard, whose existence, Snape (2011: 124) suggests, is an indication that visitors were expected in the area.

Some of these mudbrick chapels may have had their entrances walled in, which could have prevented visitors from interacting with the monuments inside. However, O'Connor (2009: 95) postulates that this could have been eased by fitting small windows that would allow for the symbolic witnessing of the festivals of Osiris. Indeed, inscriptions refer to this desire to *see* the festivals. For example, Senbef claims in an inscription on his stela (see Figure 13) that he would like to 'see the lord of the horizon as he sails across the sky' (Vienna Kunsthistorisches Museum ÄS 109). Remarkably, this stela features niches with mummiform figures in raised relief as well as an openwork ankh on its surface, which would provide a 'window' between worlds to facilitate communication between the dedicatee, the god, and also a potential audience. Senbef then goes on to say that he has built a chapel at the Terrace of the Great God in order to 'smell the incense that comes forth, in order to be provided with the sweet smell of the god'. These references to seeing the god, as well as smelling the incense are pointing at sensory perceptions of the landscape of Abydos. As I have argued in Section 3, phenomenological experiences of landscape have a significant impact on the enactment of memory.

Speaking of an audience, many stelae would feature appeals to passers-by, showing the importance of an interaction with the living, whom they try to

---

[33] Only one segment of the site has survived, as seen in Figure 11, but some chapels, such as F5-1 or F5-8, appear to have been less accessible than others. Whether this is detrimental for the dedicatee, it is difficult to say: fewer people may have seen that chapel, but perhaps they were built in that location in order to be adjacent to some powerful or influential individual, hence highlighting that connection.

Figure 13 Stela of Senbef and Ipta. Vienna Kunsthistorisches Museum ÄS 109
(© KHM-Museumsverband)

persuade to recite an invocation offering in the memory of the person who
erected the stela, as we saw with the example of Wahysobek in Section 3.3 (see
Figure 6). The role of appeals to the living has been discussed earlier; at this
point it is worth noting that these intended interactions could potentially have
been more aspirational than actual, but the fact that a hypothetical engagement
with an audience is requested is still quite significant. It is this relational quality,
this interaction with and between monuments, that actively constructs and
perpetuates spaces of memory.

So far I have presented some potential technologies of remembrance in
relation to theories of embodiment. The interactions between audience, monument, and dedicatee noted on stelae from Abydos reproduce and reflect those

performative as well as embodied aspects of commemoration: wandering around chapels, crouching to gain access to a stela, squatting to admire the images, the physical act of setting up a stela, listening to a recitation of an inscription, seeing surrounding monuments, smelling the scent of incense offerings. These are all bodily practices that, in Connerton's (1989: 39) terms, contributed to the iterative formation of memory.

Abydene stelae are an example of social engagement with objects linked to a particular space, and their essence can only be understood in light of the role they played in the celebrations of the festivities of Osiris and people's desires to participate in them through their presence on the monuments, as well as their sensory engagement with their physical and social setting. In Section 4.3, I focus on one specific ANOC group in order to show in further detail how these technologies of remembrance may have worked in practice. As previously explained, it is impossible to reconstruct the archaeological context of this area of Abydos, so this cluster of monuments is hypothetical and based on internal inscriptional and pictorial evidence. The ultimate location of this chapel at Abydos, if it ever existed, cannot be discerned, but the way it created a symbolic space of remembrance adds to our explorations of memory at Abydos.

4.3 Materialising Memory: The Chapel of Nefernay as Case Study

A detailed case study will help us understand how technologies of remembrance work in the enactment of commemoration within the landscape of Abydos, and particularly in its votive zone. For the purposes of this exercise, I have chosen ANOC 44, a group that was identified by Simpson on the basis of prosopography. The stelae that form this group were all retrieved from or attributed to Abydos, but, like most monuments from this site, they have no known archaeological context recorded. As I argue next, this lack of specific archaeological provenance makes the reconstruction of the chapel hypothetical, but the connection of these stelae to the ritual landscape of Abydos remains one of their essential characteristics. The strategies of commemoration that they display can be analysed through inscriptional and pictorial evidence, indicating that this chapel was actively creating a space of memory.

4.3.1 ANOC 44: On Style and Prosopography

ANOC 44 is a group of stelae where a man called Nefernay is presented as the main dedicatee. Simpson (1974: 20, pl. 63) ascribed three stelae to this group, namely Munich Gl. WAF 34 (ANOC 44.1; see Figure 14),[34] Florence 2590

---

[34] See https://pnm.uni-mainz.de/4/inscription/1108 (accessed 13 March 2024).

Figure 14 Stela of Nefernay, ANOC 44.1. Munich State Museum of Egyptian Art, Gl. WAF 34, Loan Wittelsbacher Ausgleichsfonds; photo: Roy Hessing

(ANOC 44.2; see Figure 15),[35] and Louvre C 206 (ANOC 44.3; see Figure 16).[36] The link between these stelae is made on the basis of personal names and titles, which could be regarded as a weak argument, but in this case the name of the dedicatee is sufficiently uncommon for this identification to merit consideration.[37] There are other monuments that could provide

---

[35] See https://pnm.uni-mainz.de/4/inscription/429 (accessed 13 March 2024).

[36] See https://pnm.uni-mainz.de/4/inscription/1109 (accessed 13 March 2024).

[37] Only five occurrences of this name are attested from this time period: https://pnm.uni-mainz.de/4/name/1642 (accessed 13 March 2024).

Figure 15 Stela of Nefernay, ANOC 44.2. Florence Museo Archeologico 2590
(Su concessione del Ministero della Cultura – Museo Archeologico Nazionale
di Firenze – Direzione regionale Musei Nazionali Toscana-Firenze)

Figure 16 Stela of Nefernay, ANOC 44.3. Paris, Musée du Louvre C206
[E.3905] © 2007 Musée du Louvre, Dist. GrandPalaisRmn/Christian Décamps
Permalink: https://collections.louvre.fr/ark:/53355/cl010022059

complementary information about some of the individuals depicted on this
group. In particular, stela Leiden AP 41,[38] which features a man named Hori
together with his son, the ỉmy-ḫt sꜣ-prw Hori.[39] A man with the same name and
titles is also depicted on the bottom register of ANOC 44.3. Another stela to

---

[38] See https://pnm.uni-mainz.de/4/inscription/2058 (accessed 13 March 2024).

[39] Another monument that could perhaps include a mention of this same man is a damaged statue
fragment studied by Vernus (1973).

consider here is Saffron Walden 1892.49, which features the man Sobekherhab and his mother Tity (Stefanović 2010; Ilin-Tomich 2014: 144). Sobekherhab is depicted in ANOC 44.1, and a woman called Tity is mentioned in ANOC 44.1 and ANOC 44.3 (although it is uncertain whether both attestations refer to the same woman). These connections between monuments point towards a thick network of social relations that is materialised within these Abydene chapels, even if they cannot be reconstructed with certainty.

ANOC 44 is dated to the early 13th dynasty on stylistic grounds.[40] These three stelae are stylistically very similar, which is why Simpson (1974: 4, n. 25) already proposed that they could have been made in the same workshop. This resemblance is shown by the shape of the faces, the short beards, the square profile of the hands, and the layout with two coloured bands at the bottom. In addition, the lunettes of ANOC 44.1 and 44.2 are almost identical, with two recumbent jackals, two shen-rings, and figures of Min-Hor-Nakht and Ptah-Sokar-Osiris.[41] Ilin-Tomich (2017), in his work on stelae workshops of the late Middle Kingdom, also notes a number of features that allow him to narrow down this workshop to his 'Memphis-Faiyum Region'. In this case, the connection of ANOC 44.1 and stela Saffron Walden 1892.49 through the man Sobekherhab mentioned in the previous paragraph is crucial. He assigns the latter stela to his '13th Dyn. Memphis-Faiyum Workshop 4' on the basis the shapes of some vessels and the spelling of some words (Ilin-Tomich 2017: 89–90), as well as the use of personal names attributed to the Memphis-Faiyum region, such as Snefru (Ilin-Tomich 2017: 52–3). By virtue of that personal link through Sobekherhab, a Memphis-Faiyum region origin is postulated for ANOC 44.1 as well.

All three stelae in this group are relatively small, ranging from 56 to 61 cm tall. Nefernay is presented in a prominent position, with four to six further individuals depicted and captioned in other registers of the stelae. A common feature to all of these captions is that none of them includes any kinship terms, a striking characteristic upon which I comment further next.

Nefernay holds the title iꜣry pḏt, often translated as 'bowman' (Stefanović 2006). This is a relatively low-ranking military title whose popularity grew

---

[40] Franke (1984: dossier 309) suggested a date around the reign of Sobekhotep IV for this ANOC group. Ilin-Tomich agrees with this 13th-dynasty dating, postulating that ANOC 44.3 should be dated more specifically to the time of treasurer Senbi, namely between the reigns of Neferhotep I and Sobekhotep IV: https://pnm.uni-mainz.de/4/inscription/1108 (accessed 13 March 2024).

[41] Stela Leiden AP 41, although similar overall, presents stylistic differences, such as the straightness of the seated figures in contrast to the slightly forward shoulders of ANOC 44.1 and ANOC 44.2. Grajetzki (2000: 165) has convincingly argued that Leiden AP 41 should be seen as part of a larger group fashioned in a different workshop possibly under Sobekhotep III, and this has been confirmed by the work of Ilin-Tomich (2012).

during the later Middle Kingdom (Awad 2004: 61; Stefanović 2005: 75). On ANOC 44.3 he has an additional title, namely šms skr, 'follower of Sokar',[42] which Fischer (1996: 105) interprets as an expression of a close relationship with local gods, as also indicated by the depiction of Ptah-Sokar-Osiris in the lunette of ANOC 44.1 and ANOC 44.2.[43] The person depicted in the most salient position in ANOC 44.1 next to Nefernay is a wet-nurse whose filiation is not given (see Section 4.3.2 on the title mnꜥt).

The social background of the rest of people featured in this group is quite varied.[44] Even though all figures are captioned, some of them do not have a title (e.g., Senbet on the bottom register of ANOC 44.2). Others hold low-ranking titles, such as šms, 'follower' (e.g., Djaa, on the bottom register of ANOC 44.1). Finally, high-ranking titles are also featured, such as ḫtmty-bïty, 'royal seal-bearer' (e.g., Sobekherhab on the second register of ANOC 44.1). Sometimes, Middle Kingdom stelae gather individuals holding titles that indicate a shared occupation; for example, workers of the necropolis or sculptors (Olabarria 2020b: 29, 123–6). This does not seem to be the case of ANOC 44, where we witness the use of titles pertaining to a variety of professional domains and hierarchical rankings. A few individuals are in supervisory positions, such as ïmy-rꜣ n ḥrtyw-nt̠r, 'overseer of the phylae of stonemasons' (see ANOC 44.2, Ka on the bottom register) or ïmy-rꜣ mšꜥ wr, 'great overseer of the troops' (see ANOC 44.1, Sobekherhab on the second register). Others, however, are simply captioned as ꜥḥꜥ, 'attendant' (see ANOC 44.1, Renseneb on the second register). Thus, it is uncertain why these people, who are not explicitly connected genealogically and who do not share a common occupation, would have been represented together on a monument intended for public display.

4.3.2 Image and Hierarchy

The filiation of Nefernay is not indicated anywhere within the group, which is why Awad (2004: 64) avoids including Nefernay within his proposed genealogical reconstruction of people in ANOC 44. Stefanović (2005: 80–1, no. 18; 2006: 172, no. 919) proposes that his mother could be a woman named Henut or Tity because these names occur on both ANOC 44.1 and 44.3. However, this connection remains hypothetical, and kin relations are not at all foregrounded in

---

[42] The term šms has been interpreted as a military title, but Stefanović (2008b) notes that individuals holding this title were in service in a variety of offices, from all administrative sectors and also from temples, and covering a wide range of duties.

[43] The allusion to these Lower Egyptian gods would support Ilin-Tomich's (2017) proposal that these stelae are related to a 'Memphis-Faiyum Region' workshop.

[44] It is very difficult to assess class and rank, especially on the basis of formalised titles and much work remains to be done on the understanding of administrative and social hierarchies of the Middle Kingdom. For some introductory discussions, see Grajetzki (2010) and Quirke (2004).

this particular example. Although some filiations are given, indicating the names of the mothers of some individuals represented in the bottom registers, no kinship terms precede their names, so their personal relationship to Nefernay is obviously not the focus of their presentation.

Something that we can observe from the way individuals are represented on the stelae of ANOC 44 is that, beyond the obvious iconographic primacy of Nefernay himself, all other characters are depicted in relatively equal terms. The only exception is the woman Nebiderenkha in ANOC 44.1,[45] who is shown at a table laden with offerings opposite Nefernay. Anne Millard (1976: vol. 2, 311–2) suggested that this representation is so unusual that Nebiderenkha must be Nefernay's wife, even though she is not captioned as such. However, there are other examples from Middle Kingdom stelae where a similar position was occupied by, for example, a collateral relative, so there is no evidence to support Millard's claim.

It is uncertain why Nebiderenkha would take such a relevant role in this monument; it could be because Nefernay wanted to highlight and honour their personal relationship, or it could be because she had an important role that Nefernay would benefit from displaying. She holds the title mnꜥt, often translated as 'wet-nurse' (Rodríguez-Berzosa Gómez-Landero 2016: 535–1073). Much of the scholarship on non-royal wet-nurses in Egypt deals with Demotic and Greek evidence (e.g., Strauss 2018); however, there are some attestations that can be dated back to earlier periods, with particular emphasis on the Middle Kingdom.[46] Stefanović (2008a) records 78 attestations of women bearing the title mnꜥt in Middle Kingdom sources, arguing that they were mainly female house attendants. Kasparian (2007) reviews the important role of wet-nurses in the Middle Kingdom, and he proposes that they would be regarded as part of the kin group. Although this is not explicitly mentioned in any texts, the visual vocabulary of display indicates that this could well be the case, with women like Nebiderenkha being presented in a position that would often be reserved to family.[47] With this notable exception, all other figures in ANOC 44.1 are very similar iconographically, which may lead some to argue that those individuals are presented as peers.

As seen in Section 4.3.1, however, people displayed in ANOC 44 held titles that point at vast hierarchical gaps among them in terms of rank. These stark

[45] See https://pnm.uni-mainz.de/4/name/1953 (accessed 12 April 2024).
[46] For a general study on nursing and breastfeeding, see Rodríguez-Berzosa Gómez-Landero (2016). For New Kingdom evidence, see Cannon Fairbairn's ongoing research on breastfeeding (PhD at University of Birmingham).
[47] Kasparian (2007: 121) suggests that stelae ANOC 44.1 could actually be dedicated to both of them, given the prominent position of Nebiderenkha.

differences are only perceivable from the reading of the captions, not from the depictions themselves. I have studied these conventions of 'undifferentiated' depictions elsewhere (Olabarria 2012: 890–3), concluding that beneath the allegedly egalitarian appearance of these characters, the main role of monumental representation is to reinforce and highlight the primacy of the dedicatee. Hence, ANOC 44 affirms the importance of Nefernay by presenting him as a person with multiple connections.

The question at this point would be why those people from vastly different social backgrounds were brought together on ANOC 44. It could be that this group should be contemplated as a networking tool rather than a cluster of monuments commemorating a family. Other examples of monument clusters used to materialise and commemorate networking are known, for example, from the sanctuary of Heqaib in Elephantine (for further examples, see Olabarria 2020b: 128–30; 143–53). These stelae show relationships that are manipulated and reinterpreted in order to convey a message of status by means of the visual vocabulary of relatedness.

Many stelae of the Middle Kingdom, especially from the late Middle Kingdom, show collaterals represented in very similar poses and sizes (Olabarria 2020b: 29, 54–6). In those cases, we know what role they play because they are captioned as sn or its female counterpart snt, a kinship term that could be used for what in anthropology of kinship would be understood as a 'collateral'. These relationships would involve at least one 'horizontal' connection if represented in a genealogical diagram, hence encompassing siblings, aunts and uncles, nieces and nephews, and other relatives from several generations (Olabarria 2020b: 63–7). In the case of ancient Egyptian kinship terminology, the term sn was exceptionally encompassing, and it could also include colleagues, friends, neighbours, and other members of the extended family. An example of the typical use of the term sn in late Middle Kingdom monuments would be the stela of Ibu (Cairo CG 20722; Lange and Schäfer 1902b: pl. liv; Olabarria 2020b: 29), where dozens of people are depicted and captioned as sn, probably all belonging to the same workshop of sculptors.[48] Some scholars have regarded this proliferation of people captioned as sn on stelae in the late Middle Kingdom as a revalorisation of relations of collaterality (Grajetzki 2007; Nelson-Hurst 2010), but I see it rather as way of exalting the individuality of ego, characterising him (less often her) as someone with a large social entourage.

The main difference between many other late Middle Kingdom stelae and those of Nefernay is that the latter do not feature the term sn explicitly. There are

---

[48] On artists, sculptors, and workshops in the Middle Kingdom, see Quirke (2003), Stefanović (2012), Connor (2020: 243–52), and Ilin-Tomich (2017).

other examples of late Middle Kingdom stelae where kinship terms are conspicuously absent (e.g., Cairo CG 20520; Lange and Schäfer 1902b: pl. xxxvi; Simpson 1974: pl. 50 [ANOC 32.1]), which, of course, leaves it to the imagination of the audience to decide how those people were related. I would argue that even though the term sn is not being used in these examples, perhaps a relation of collaterality is being evoked by analogy with similar stelae of the same period. The audiences of these monuments would probably be able to identify those represented as collaterals on the basis of a shared social knowledge of what a collateral may appear like on stelae, that is to say, as a result of being members of the same mnemonic community.

As introduced in Section 3, Valerie Hope (2000: esp. 156) has referred to this way of conveying social information in the Roman context as a 'rhetoric of commemoration' that provides an idealistic representation about the identity of an individual or a group that should not be taken at face value. For her, such a rhetoric of commemoration would include visual as well as linguistic components, respectively a 'rhetoric of images' and a 'rhetoric of language'. In this case, this undifferentiated depiction would exemplify that rhetoric of images at play in the monumental record of Middle Kingdom Abydos, as the local conventions of representation need to be known in order to make social sense of those monuments. Visual references that are elusive to us would have been self-evident to those socialised into this culture of display. This use of a particular representational strategy to convey a message, in this case a message of status, is an example of what, following Andrew Jones, I have been calling 'technologies of remembrance'.

4.3.3 Appeals and Interaction

Audience is a fundamental consideration when thinking of the roles that stelae from Abydos play on memorialisation. It should be regarded as having an active role in these processes, as interaction was required in order for remembrance to be activated. Audience, be it mortal or divine, material or human, present or future, establishes and perpetuates an active dialogue with the monumental record of the site, bringing relationality to the forefront.

For example, in ANOC 44.2 the audience is addressed explicitly through an elaborate appeal to the living. This appeal to the living is carved in large hieroglyphs in eight columns on the upper half of the stela. The signs themselves are about three times larger than those in the lower registers, where four people are depicted with much smaller captions. This differential treatment of the inscriptions makes the appeal to the living the undeniable focus of this composition. This is also worth bearing in mind given the features of the landscape of the Terrace of the Great God that I outline in Section 4.2. The votive zone of Abydos would have been characterised by competitive display; hence, any attempt to draw attention to one monument or a part of it should be given its due importance.

In terms of contents, the inscription is a prime example of how interaction with a potential audience can be prompted in writing. Here I provide a translation of the whole appeal in ANOC 44.2 (columns 1–8).

> He says: O living ones upon earth, every scribe, every lector priest,
> every official who shall pass by this chapel, as you desire that Osiris,
> the lord of life, the ruler of eternity, endures for you, may you say 1000
> bread and beer, 1000 oxen and fowl, 1000 offerings and provisions,
> upon the offering table of the lord of eternity for the ka of the overseer
> of bowmen Nefernay, because it is more beneficial
> for the one who acts than for the one for whom one acts. The breath of
> the mouth is beneficial for the deceased. One does not
> become weary because of it. I am
> a deceased to whom one should listen,
> as there is a good reward for the one who does it.

The appeal features assertive phrases that emphasise the importance of reciprocity. For example, the expression 'the breath of the mouth is beneficial for the deceased. One does not become weary because of it' is known from the so-called breath of the mouth formula. This phrase was known from the Middle Kingdom onwards, but it became particularly popular during the 25th dynasty. Vernus (1976; see also Spiegelberg 1908) compiled all known Middle Kingdom attestations of this formula, and he linked them to other forms of expressions of reciprocity as known from didactic literature. The composition of the appeal is nonetheless highly formulaic, possibly seeking a connection with similar language found in elite sources. Comparable affirmations of the moral standing of an individual are also known from self-presentation texts from as early as the Old Kingdom (Stauder-Porchet 2017: 179–208; 2020: 90–6; see also Lichtheim 1992: esp. 12–3), and they harken back to Jan Assmann's notion of ma'at as a principle that guides this reciprocal interaction with ancestors, advanced in Section 3.1. This is particularly relevant for our case study, as the inscription on ANOC 44.2 ends also with an affirmation of the good character of Nefernay by stating that 'I am a deceased to whom one should listen, as there is a good reward for the one who does it'.

Many promises of a reward are known from Egyptian appeals to the living, something that emphasises the performative and interactive quality of the monuments on which they are inscribed. For example, in Section 3.1 I presented the Middle Kingdom stela of Montuhotep (Cairo CG 20539), with an inscription that reads 'as for the one who will remember my good name, I shall be his protector'. Expressions such as this one reiterate the benefits that performing an invocation offering and perpetuating the memory of the deceased would entail, but they also raise questions about the literacy of those interacting with the monument. As noted in Section 3, considerations of literacy are crucial, but these monuments also had other ways of enticing interaction that did not necessarily rely on the viewers' ability to read fluently.

Another important point noted by Shubert (2007: 426) is that these formulaic expressions imply the apparent ability to recite invocation offerings. Sometimes ḥtp-dỉ-nswt formulae and variation thereof are fully written on the stelae (as in the case of ANOC 44.2), which reiterates the problems regarding literacy mentioned earlier. In other cases, inscriptions only demand of the reader that an invocation offering be recited, without providing the actual text of such invocation written out. This indicates the presumption of a shared cultural identity and social knowledge, the recognition of a mnemonic community, by virtue of which any individual asked to pronounce an invocation offering would know exactly what that may entail. This conception of shared cultural identity is linked to the characterisations of relational memory that I have proposed in previous paragraphs: memory can be anchored in the iteration of rituals, and the recitations alluded to on these texts would be part of them.

While the pictorial treatment explored in the previous section exemplifies a rhetoric of images, here we see a rhetoric of language that makes use of stock phrases and formulaic expressions to invite different actors to perform memory. An elaborate appeal to the living such as this one reinforces a desire to engage with an audience, creating a space that is both physical and symbolic, as I propose in Section 4.3.4.

4.3.4 Space and the Anchoring of Memory

The final element that I would like to explore with this case study is how these stelae may anchor remembrance to a particular place. Although a precise archaeological contextualisation is not possible due to the history of the site, the chapel that the stelae in ANOC 44 may have belonged to was conceived as a discrete unit of memorialisation. As discussed earlier, inscriptions demonstrate that stelae were conceived as components of mꜥḥꜥt-chapels, hence showing that a symbolic as well as physical space for commemoration was being demarcated.

However, the stelae of Nefernay do not include the word mꜥḥꜥt. Instead, the inscription on ANOC 44.2 refers to the monument that bears the inscription as a šps. Different terms for stela have been identified in Middle Kingdom sources, namely ꜥbꜣ, wḏ, srḫ, and of course šps.[49] A close analysis demonstrates that the use of a given term does not depend on physical shape of the object, but probably on their intended function.

Two main purposes can be associated with stelae termed šps (Olabarria 2020a: 132–6). First, they were meant to be displayed. This is exemplified by inscriptions such as a stela of a certain Senpu, now in Toulouse (see Figures 17a and 17b), which reads 'o living ones, every wab-priest, every scribe, every lector priest, who will see this šps, as you praise Ptah, you will leave your offices to your children' (Toulouse 49.274; Ramond 1977: 5–9, pl. ii; Simpson 1974: pl. 74 [ANOC 55.4]). This text emphasises that sensory experience of *seeing* a monument alluded to in Section 4.2. It is implied that seeing the stela would entail a reciprocal action of commemoration that will be beneficial both to the audience and to the people represented on the stela. Moreover, it should be noted that the inscription in this example is not carved on the main surface, but on one of the edges of the stela. Since it is an appeal to the living, with which the audience was expected to interact, one should assume that the inscription should have been visible, hence giving us an indication of location and directionality. Perhaps this stela was set up close to a processional route at Abydos, and at a self-standing location that would allow any text on the edge to be visible.[50]

Second, the majority of stelae that include self-referential mentions as šps are associated with appeals to the living (Olabarria 2020a: 158–62). These appeals, as explained in Section 4.3.3, foreground the desire for interaction with the audience, asking all the living ones to recite invocation offerings in the memory of the person for whom the stela was erected and their social group. Hence, the term šps denotes that this object was meant to be interacted with, which supports the idea that it was erected close to processional routes in the ritual landscape of Abydos to maximise contact with passers-by. Perhaps these intended inter-actions with an audience should be understood as an attempt to create a space of memory sustained by those whose actions were prompted by these inscrip-tions, even if the specific delineation of a physical place is not known to us from archaeological sources.

Place-making as a symbolic as well as physical process also has a crucial temporal dimension. Chapels were probably not built as bounded units, and they could have had components added to them over time by individuals and groups

---

[49] See Olabarria (2020a) for a detailed discussion on terminology for stelae in the Middle Kingdom.

[50] I have also argued how the use of the O20 shrine determinative in the writing of šps may corroborate this proposed location, as that determinative could be associated with directional rows of monuments, something that would make sense in the ritual landscape of Abydos (Olabarria 2020a: 136).

(a)   (b)

Figures 17a and 17b Stela of Senpu, ANOC 55.4. Toulouse 49.274 (after
Ramond 1977: pl. ii)

seeking to materialise social connections at the site.[51] In addition, the distribution of chapels as seen in Figure 11 probably indicates that smaller spaces in-
between larger chapels could have been progressively filled in a way that would
have shaped the dynamics of engagement with those monuments, impacting on
the nature of performative interaction at the site. All of this draws attention to
the fact that performative interaction with these spaces should not be regarded
as static and frozen in time, but productively analysed through the framework of

---

[51] For an example of a chapel that could have been built element by element over a number of years,
see Olabarria (forthcoming), with a discussion of ANOC 1.

genealogies of place, namely as a spaces that gain meaning and have their significance continuously reworked over time.

Overall, I believe ANOC 44 is an illustrative case study to showcase possible ways of articulating Jones' technologies of remembrance with the monumental record of Middle Kingdom Abydos. In this section I have argued that the stelae of Nefernay display three main aspects of memory. First, ANOC 44 shows a group that is commemorated together while relying on the social knowledge of the audience to interpret relationships celebrated on these monuments. The presence of certain people is more important than labelling their relationships accurately, and those relationships are only hinted at by the way they are displayed. The connection between those people represented on ANOC 44 is not clear through captions, but the visual vocabulary of the stelae helps interpret their relationship on the basis of shared social knowledge and memory. This is what I have referred to mainly as a rhetoric of images. Second, these stelae address the audience by means of an explicit appeal that prompts performative action on the part of the viewers. This rhetoric of language relies on common social knowledge that facilitates the enactment of remembrance. Third, ANOC 44 creates a physical and/or symbolic space to prompt the celebration of memory by virtue of those interactions. As such, this case study demonstrates that objects are not memory, but that they operate within those networks of relations.

4.4 Tracing Memory at Abydos

In this section, I have explored stelae from Abydos as commemorative monuments that must have been affected by contemporary understandings of social structure. In my approach, however, I take chapels, and not individual stelae as the foci of memory, because Egyptian inscriptions demonstrate that chapels can be regarded as bounded units. Memorial chapels construct and materialise relationships that are perpetuated in the memory of contemporary visitors and of generations to come. In this sense, chapels can be regarded as a microcosm of memory, since they make use of various technologies of remembrance, in the sense advanced by Andrew Jones, on a small scale in order to sustain social ideas.

In this section I have used one group of stelae, namely ANOC 44, as a case study to explore different aspects of memory. For example, the absence of concrete kinship terms shows that the genealogical position of those present was less important than the fact that they were present. The idea of collaterality permeated stelae that focused on display of status and authority even when collaterality was not explicitly mentioned. It also shows how a group could be commemorated together by sharing space in the monumental record, while relying on the knowledge of the audience in order to interpret the relationships celebrated on them.

One of the things I have argued in this Element is that definitions of memory need to be contingent and context-bound. Some of the previous models were relying on computational approaches, on unidirectional transmission of units of knowledge, or on hermeneutical exercises over textual sources. Based on the discussions of Abydos as a site of memory and as illustrated through the case study of Nefernay, I propose a fourfold definition of memory instead: memory is situated, embodied, performative, and actively constructed. Memory at Abydos is situated because the role of stelae and chapels is embedded in the landscape, and this is exemplified by their interaction with that processional route. It is embodied because personal sensory aspirations, such as the desire to see the festivals, played an important role in the objects' engagement with viewers and with the landscape. It is performative because interaction with passers-by, who can be explicitly requested to recite invocation offerings, is required for that reinforcement of memory. Finally, it is actively constructed because groups commemorated on these stelae and memorial chapels may not have existed as such in lived experience, but they were still presented on stelae as meaningful social groups. Memory was both prompted by the actors and expected from the audience for a full realisation of remembrance, so overall it is fair to say that memory is not passive, but rather actively constructed.

5 Making Memories about Ancient Egypt

This Element has focused on how people remembered in Middle Kingdom Egypt, and in these concluding remarks I would like to reflect on some of the wider implications of the ideas advanced in it. In particular, I am interested in how the making of those memories should not be relegated to the past but, as hinted at in previous sections, continues to be relevant in the present.

The uses of materiality and the emergence of memory out of networks of relationships in the past have been the main theoretical approach of this Element. Memory should not be seen as something that lies dormant in things, but as an aspect that is co-created in a dynamic and practical way. I have underlined the uses of performativity in the context of Middle Kingdom Abydos in order to bring attention to interactions with monuments in the construction and enactment of memory. Materiality and performativity are here assessed in relation to the study of ancient Egypt, and memory is presented as something that continues to be reworked and actively constructed over time.

An aspect that I have not considered in detail, however, is how ancient Egypt is remembered. Here I am not only referring to ideas of reception and reimaginings of Egypt in modern times, a topic that is gaining momentum in academic Egyptology, but rather to the fact that the material vestiges of Egypt that I have used in previous sections to characterise the practice of memory are being studied from the present and through present understandings.

Archaeology undeniably studies the remains of the past in the present, and the role and impact of this multi-scalar move has been noted and problematised in archaeological theory from various perspectives. The present, archaeologist Laurent Olivier (2004: 205) claims, is multi-temporal, as it is made up of material things that survive from the past and gain meaning from present interpretations. In that same article, Olivier (2004: 212) goes on to describe, for example, how in Paris the ancient Roman *decumanus* survives in the guise of a modern boulevard, which is effectively a memory of the ancient urban fabric of the city. This is an example of how different temporalities converge, and memory of the past becomes a memory in the present.[52] In other words, to *do* archaeology is to *perform* memory.

While there is a clear analytical difference between commemorating people in the past and reimagining a society from the present, I am interested in the opportunities and challenges that the latter practice may afford. Reception provides a stimulating and insightful way to think about forms of the past in the present. Reception studies, as an academic discipline, establishes the need to set a frame of reference rather than assume that the contexts of the past are fixed and self-explanatory; it considers how ideas about the past have been perceived, transmitted, and reinterpreted. This emphasis on the significance of representation and interpretation – rather than a futile search for a single truth – draws attention to the roles of the communities of practice involved. In this manner, reception helps raise awareness about the constructed nature of our knowledge about ancient Egypt, which is mediated by concerns about the present, providing a unique opportunity to reflect on ourselves and to deliver new insights about Egypt in general. If, as I have argued in this Element, memories are contextual, contingent, and actively constructed, the ways in which ancient Egypt is represented today serve as witnesses to a dialogue that has been established with the past. Thus, to reimagine Egypt may also be regarded as a way to perform memory.

---

[52] Oliver Harris (2021: 106–8) has warned against the risks of establishing a conceptual dichotomy between archaeology-as-memory and archaeology-as-history: on the one hand, it is important to acknowledge change through time; on the other, we should not impose any extraneous forms of temporalities on the materials that we study. Instead, Harris (2021: 109–16) advocates for the potential of process philosophy, with an emphasis on the notion of emergence, in order to nuance archaeological articulations of the idea of time.

In this Element, I have tried to account for a multi-temporal perspective that considers not simply how commemoration may have operated in the past, but also how it is perceived and understood from the perspective of the present. By proposing a model of how memories were made in Middle Kingdom Abydos, I have described dynamic changes that can be perceived in the monumental record that contributed to fostering different genealogies of place. These include the progressive addition to memorial chapels, and the accumulation of subsequent layers of meaning that added to the potent symbolism of the site of Abydos. Technologies of remembrance have been introduced as an interpretative framework that focuses on ancient and modern engagements with monuments. On the one hand, they recognise how performative interaction was one of the keys to the enactment of commemoration in this historical context. On the other, the distribution of stelae across museum collections around the world has led to a segmentation of memory that can only be bridged through a consideration of the past through the present. These interrelated temporalities need to be combined to grasp the complexities of this material world and understand the processes of remembering that they display. I have argued that memory at Middle Kingdom Abydos was situated, embodied, performative, and actively constructed, and I have invited the reader to rethink what this means from a past as well as a present perspective.

References

Adams, Matthew Douglas. 2019. 'The origins of sacredness at Abydos', in Ilona Regulski (ed.), *Abydos: The sacred land at the western horizon* (Peeters: Leuven), 25–70.

Agnew, John A. 1987. *Place and politics: The geographical mediation of state and society* (Allen & Unwin: Boston, MA).

Alcock, Susan E. 2002. *Archaeologies of the Greek past: Landscape, monuments, and memories* (Cambridge University Press: Cambridge).

Alvarez, Christelle, and Yegor Grebnev. 2022. 'Approaching monumentality in pre-modern epigraphic and manuscript traditions', *Manuscript and Text Cultures* 1: 1–10.

Amélineau, Émile. 1899. *Le tombeau d'Osiris: monographie de la découverte faite en 1897–1898* (Ernest Leroux: Paris).

Assmann, Aleida. 2010a. 'Canon and archive', in Astrid Erll and Ansgar Nünning (eds.), *A companion to cultural memory studies* (De Gruyter: Berlin), 97–108.

—— 2011a. *Cultural memory and Western civilization: Functions, media, archives* (Cambridge University Press: Cambridge).

Assmann, Jan. 1988. 'Stein und Zeit: das "monumentale" Gedächtnis der altägyptischen Kultur', in Jan Assmann and Tonio Hölscher (eds.), *Kultur und Gedächtnis* (Suhrkamp: Frankfurt am Main), 87–114.

—— 1991. *Stein und Zeit: Mensch und Gesellschaft im alten Ägypten* (Fink: München).

—— 2002 [1996]. *The mind of Egypt: History and meaning in the time of the pharaohs*. Translated by Andrew Jenkins (Holt: New York).

—— 2006. 'Form as a mnemonic device: Cultural texts and cultural memory', in Richard A. Horsley, Jonathan A. Draper, and John Miles Foley (eds.), *Performing the gospel: Orality, memory, and mark: Essays dedicated to Werner Kelber* (Fortress: Minneapolis, MN), 67–82.

—— 2010b. 'Communicative and cultural memory', in Astrid Erll and Ansgar Nünning (eds.), *A companion to cultural memory studies* (De Gruyter: Berlin), 109–18.

—— 2011b. *Cultural memory and early civilization: Writing, remembrance, and political imagination* (Cambridge University Press: Cambridge).

Atkinson, Richard C., and Richard M. Shiffrin. 1968. 'Human memory: A proposed system and its control processes,' in Kenneth W. Spence and

Janet T. Spence (eds.), *The psychology of learning and motivation: Advances in research and theory* (Academic Press: New York), 89–195.

Awad, Khaled Ahmed Hamza. 2004. 'Die Abydos-Stele des Nfr-nA-jj aus dem Mittleren Reich', *Göttinger Miszellen* 199: 61–6.

Baines, John. 1990. 'Restricted knowledge, hierarchy and decorum: Modern perceptions and ancient institutions', *Journal of the American Research Center in Egypt* 27: 1–23.

2006. 'Public ceremonial performance in ancient Egypt: Exclusion and integration', in Takeshi Inomata and Lawrence S. Coben (eds.), *Archaeology of performance: Theaters of power, community, and politics* (AltaMira: Lanham, MD), 261–302.

Baines, John, and Christopher J. Eyre. 2007. 'Four notes on literacy', in John Baines (ed.), *Visual and written culture in ancient Egypt* (Oxford University Press: Oxford), 63–94.

Barbiera, Irene, Alice M. Choyke, and Judith A. Rasson (eds). 2009. *Materializing memory: Archaeological material culture and the semantics of the past* (Archaeopress: Oxford).

Beckerath, Jürgen von. 1992. 'Zur Geschichte von Chonsemḥab und dem Geist', *Zeitschrift für Ägyptische Sprache und Altertumskunde* 119: 90–107.

Bernbeck, Reinhard, Kerstin P. Hofmann, and Ulrike Sommer. 2017. 'Mapping memory, space and conflict', in Reinhard Bernbeck, Kerstin P. Hofmann, and Ulrike Sommer (eds.), *Between memory sites and memory networks: New archaeological and historical perspectives* (Edition Topoi/ Exzellenzcluster Topoi der Freien Universität Berlin und der Humboldt-Universität zu Berlin: Berlin), 9–32.

Bloch, Maurice. 1971. *Placing the dead: Tombs, ancestral villages, and kinship organization in Madagascar* (Seminar Press: London).

Boivin, Nicole. 2008. *Material cultures, material minds: The impact of things on human thought, society, and evolution* (Cambridge University Press: Cambridge).

Borić, Dušan. 2010. 'Introduction: Memory, archaeology and the historical condition', in Dušan Borić (ed.), *Archaeology and memory* (Oxbow Books: Oxford), 1–34.

Bradley, Richard. 1998. *The significance of monuments: On shaping of human experience in Neolithic and Bronze Age Europe* (Routledge: London).

2002. *The past in prehistoric societies* (Routledge: London).

Brigard, Felipe, Sharda Umanath, and Muireann Irish (eds) 2022. Special Issue: Rethinking the distinction between episodic and semantic memory. *Memory & Cognition* 50 (3): 459–654.

Brunke, Hagan, Evelyne Bukowiecki, Eva Cancik-Kirschbaum et al. 2016. 'Thinking big: Research in monumental constructions in antiquity', *eTopoi. Journal of Ancient Studies* 6: 230–305.

Brysbaert, Ann. 2018. 'Constructing monuments, perceiving monumentality: Introduction', in Ann Brysbaert, Victor Klinkenberg, Anna Gutiérrez Garcia-M, and Irene Vikatou (eds.), *Constructing monuments, perceiving monumentality & the economics of building: Theoretical and methodological approaches to the built environment* (Sidestone Press: Leiden), 21–47.

Buccellati, Federico. 2019. 'Monumentality: Research approaches and methodology', in Federico Buccellati, Sebastian Heyden Hageneuer, Sylva van der, and Felix Levenson (eds.), *Size matters: Understanding monumentality across ancient civilizations* (transcript Verlag: Bielefeld), 41–63.

Budka, Julia. 2019. 'Umm el-Qa'ab and the sacred landscape of Abydos: New perspectives based on the votive potteyr for Osiris', in Ilona Regulski (ed.), *Abydos: The sacred land at the western horizon* (Peeters: Leuven), 85–92.

Bussmann, Richard. 2019. 'Monumentality in context: A reply from Egyptology', in Federico Buccellati, Sebastian Heyden Hageneuer, Sylva van der, and Felix Levenson (eds.), *Size matters: Understanding monumentality across ancient civilizations* (transcript Verlag: Bielefeld), 99–104.

Cahail, Kevin M. 2022. 'May your sight be open to witness Osiris: The interaction of monument, ritual, and landscape at Abydos from the First Intermediate Period to the New Kingdom', in Lara Weiss, Nico Staring, and Huw Twiston Davies (eds.), *Perspectives on lived religion II: The making of a cultural geography* (Leiden: Sidestone Press), 125–38.

Castagnoli, Luca, and Paola Ceccarelli (eds). 2019. *Greek memories: Theories and practices* (Cambridge University Press: Cambridge).

Confino, Alon. 2010. 'Memory and the history of mentalities', in Astrid Erll and Ansgar Nünning (eds.), *A companion to cultural memory studies* (De Gruyter: Berlin), 77–84.

Connerton, Paul. 1989. *How societies remember* (Cambridge University Press: Cambridge).

Connor, Simon. 2018. 'Mutiler, tuer, désactiver les images en Égypte pharaonique', *Perspective* 2: 147–66.

2020. *Être et paraître: Statues royales et privées de la fin du Moyen Empire et de la Deuxième Période intermédiaire (18501550 av .J.–C.)* (Golden House: London).

Cresswell, Tim. 2015. *Place: An introduction* (Wiley Blackwell: Chichester).

Dawkins, Richard. 1976. *The selfish gene* (Oxford University Press: Oxford).

De Meyer, Marleen. 2005. 'Restoring the tombs of his ancestors? Djehutinakht, son of Teti, at Deir al-Barsha and Sheikh Said', in Martin Fitzenreiter (ed.), *Genealogie: Realität und Fiktion von Identität. Workshop am 04. und 05. Juni 2004* (Golden House: London), 125–36.

Devlin, Zoe. 2007. *Remembering the dead in Anglo-Saxon England: Memory theory in archaeology and history* (Archaeopress: Oxford).

Di Teodoro, Micòl. 2022. 'The preservation of monuments in the written sources of Dynastic Egypt between 2000 and 1550 BC', in Gianluca Miniaci and Wolfram Grajetzki (eds.), *The world of the Middle Kingdom Egypt (2000–1550 BC): Contributions on archaeology, art, religion, and written sources* (Golden House: London), 81–99.

Dignas, Beate (ed.). 2020. *A cultural history of memory in antiquity* (Bloomsbury Academic: London).

Dignas, Beate, Roland Ralph Redfern Smith, and Simon R. F. Price (eds). 2012. *Historical and religious memory in the ancient world* (Oxford University Press: Oxford).

Dreyer, Günter. 1998. *Umm el-Qaab I: das prädynastische Königsgrab U-j und seine frühen Schriftzeugnisse* (Philipp von Zabern: Mainz).

2007. 'Abydos: The Early Dynastic royal cemetery of Umm el-Qaab', in Ute Rummel (ed.), *Meeting the past: 100 years in Egypt: German Archaeological Institute Cairo 1907–2007* (Deutsches Archäologisches Institut: Cairo), 54–94.

Effland, Andreas, and Ute Effland. 2010. '"Ritual Landscape" und "Sacred Space": Überlegungen zu Kultausrichtung und Prozessionsachsen in Abydos', *MOSAIKjournal* 1: 127–58.

2013. *Abydos: Tor zur ägyptischen Unterwelt* (Philipp von Zabern: Darmstadt).

Effland, Ute, Julia Budka, and Andreas Effland. 2010. 'Studien zum Osiriskult in Umm el-Qaab/Abydos. Ein Vorbericht', *Mitteilungen des Deutschen Archäologischen Instituts, Abteilung Kairo* 66: 19–91.

Erll, Astrid. 2010. 'Cultural memory studies: An introduction', in Astrid Erll and Ansgar Nünning (eds.), *A companion to cultural memory studies* (De Gruyter: Berlin), 1–18.

Fischer, Henry George. 1996. *Varia nova* (Metropolitan Museum of Art: New York).

Foster, Jonathan K. 2009. *Memory: A very short introduction* (Oxford University Press: Oxford).

Franke, Detlef. 1984. *Personendaten aus dem Mittleren Reich (20.-16. Jahrhundert v. Chr.): Dossiers 1–796* (O. Harrassowitz: Wiesbaden).

Gardiner, Alan H., and Kurt Sethe. 1928. *Egyptian letters to the dead, mainly from the Old and Middle Kingdoms* (Egypt Exploration Society: London).

Gedi, Noa, and Yigal Elam. 1996. 'Collective memory – What is it?', *History and Memory* 8: 30–50.

Grajetzki, Wolfram. 2000. *Die höchsten Beamten der ägyptischen Zentralverwaltung zur Zeit des Mittleren Reiches: Prosopographie, Titel und Titelreihen* (Achet: Berlin).

2007. 'Multiple burials in ancient Egypt to the end of the Middle Kingdom', in Silke Grallert and Wolfram Grajetzki (eds.), *Life and afterlife in ancient Egypt during the Middle Kingdom and Second Intermediate Period* (Golden House: London), 16–34.

2010. 'Class and society: Position and possessions', in Willeke Wendrich (ed.), *Egyptian Archaeology* (Wiley-Blackwell: Oxford), 180–99.

Guilhou, Nadine. 2021. 'Mariette à Abydos: une découverte douce-amère', *Égypte, Afrique & Orient* 103: 37–46.

Halbwachs, Maurice. 1992 [1952/1941]. *On collective memory*. Translated by Lewis A. Coser (University of Chicago Press: Chicago).

Hallam, Elizabeth, and Jennifer Hockey. 2001. *Death, memory, and material culture* (Berg: Oxford).

Hamilakis, Yannis. 2013. *Archaeology and the senses: Human experience, memory, and affect* (Cambridge University Press: New York).

2017. 'Sensorial assemblages: Affect, memory and temporality in assemblage thinking', *Cambridge Archaeological Journal* 27: 169–82.

Harris, Oliver J. T. 2021. 'Archaeology, process and time: Beyond history versus memory', *World Archaeology* 53: 104–21.

Harris, Oliver J. T., and Craig N. Cipolla. 2017. *Archaeological theory in the new millennium: Introducing current perspectives* (Routledge: London).

Harth, Dietrich. 2010. 'The invention of cultural memory', in Astrid Erll and Ansgar Nünning (eds.), *A companion to cultural memory studies* (De Gruyter: Berlin), 85–96.

Hicks, Dan. 2010. 'The material-culture turn: Event and effect', in Dan Hicks and Mary Carolyn Beaudry (eds.), *The Oxford handbook of material culture studies* (Oxford University Press: Oxford), 24–98.

Hill, Jane A. 2010. 'Window between worlds: The ankh as a dominant theme in five Middle Kingdom mortuary monuments', in Zahi Hawass and Jennifer Houser Wegner (eds.), *Millions of jubilees: Studies in honor of David P. Silverman* (Conseil Suprême des Antiquités de l'Égypte: Cairo), 227–47.

Hope, Valerie. 2000. 'Inscription and sculpture: The construction of identity in the military tombs of Roman Mainz', in Graham Oliver (ed.), *The epigraphy of death: Studies in the history and society of Greece and Rome* (Liverpool University Press: Liverpool), 155–85.

Horn, Christian, Gustav Wollentz, Gianpiero Di Maida, and Annette Haug. 2020. 'Introduction', in Christian Horn, Gustav Wollentz, Gianpiero Di Maida, and Annette Haug (eds.), *Places of memory: Spatialised practices of remembrance from prehistory to today* (Archaeopress: Oxford), 1–7.

Hsieh, Julia. 2022. *Ancient Egyptian letters to the dead: The realm of the dead through the voice of the living.* Harvard Egyptological Studies 15 (Brill: Leiden).

Huyssen, Andreas. 1995. *Twilight memories: Marking time in a culture of amnesia* (Routledge: New York).

Ilin-Tomich, Alexander. 2012. 'Late Middle Kingdom stelae workshops at Thebes', *Göttinger Miszellen* 234: 69–84.

—— 2014. 'Review: Grajetzki, Wolfram and Danijela Stefanović 2012. Dossiers of Ancient Egyptians – the Middle Kingdom and Second Intermediate Period: Addition to Franke's "Personendaten." GHP Egyptology 19. London: Golden House Publications', *Bibliotheca Orientalis* 71: 139–45.

—— 2017. *From workshop to sanctuary: The production of Late Middle Kingdom memorial stelae* (Golden House: London).

Ingold, Tim. 1993. 'The temporality of the landscape', *World Archaeology* 25: 152–74.

—— 2000a. 'Ancestry, generation, substance, memory, land', in Tim Ingold (ed.), *The perception of the environment: Essays on liverlihood, dwelling and skill* (Routledge: London), 132–51.

—— 2000b. 'Building, dwelling, living: How animals and people make themselves at home in the world', in Tim Ingold (ed.), *The perception of the environment: Essays on liverlihood, dwelling and skill* (Routledge: London), 172–88.

Jiménez-Higueras, María de los Ángeles. 2020. *The sacred landscape of Dra Abu el-Naga during the new kingdom: People making landscape making people* (Brill: Leiden).

Jiménez-Serrano, Alejandro. 2023. *Descendants of a lesser god: Regional power in Old and Middle Kingdom Egypt* (The American University in Cairo Press: Cairo).

Jones, Andrew. 2003. 'Technologies of remembrance: Memory, materiality and identity in early Bronze Age Scotland', in Howard Williams (ed.), *Archaeologies of remembrance: Death and memory in past societies* (Kluwer Academic/Plenum: New York), 65–88.

—— 2007. *Memory and material culture* (Cambridge University Press: Cambridge).

Joyce, Rosemary A. 2003. 'Concrete memories: Fragments of the past in the classic Maya present (500–1000 AD)', in Ruth M. Van Dyke and Susan E. Alcock (eds.), *Archaeologies of memory* (Blackwell: Malden, MA), 104–25.

Kasparian, Burt. 2007. 'La condition des nourrices sous le Moyen Empire', *Bulletin del Institut Français d'Archéologie Orientale* 107: 109–26.

Knappett, Carl. 2005. *Thinking through material culture: An interdisciplinary perspective* (University of Pennsylvania Press: Philadelphia).

Kopleff, Heather. 2017. 'A Community in stone: The "cenotaph" stelae of Abydos', PhD, Institute of Fine Arts, New York University.

Kucharek, Andrea. 2006. 'Die Prozession des Osiris in Abydos: zur Signifikanz archäologischer Quellen für die Rekonstruktion eines zentralen Festrituals', in Jannis Mylonopoulos and Hubert Roeder (eds.), *Archäologie und Ritual: auf der Suche nach der rituellen Handlung in den antiken Kulturen Ägyptens und Griechenlands* (Phoibos: Vienna), 53–64.

Landgráfová, Renata. 2011. *It is my good name that you should remember: Egyptian biographical texts on Middle Kingdom stelae* (Faculty of Arts, Charles University in Prague; Czech Institute of Egyptology).

Lange, H. O. 1896. 'Zwei Inschriften der Fürsten von Hermonthis', *Zeitschrift für Ägyptische Sprache und Altertumskunde* 34: 25–35.

Lange, H. O., and Heinrich Schäfer. 1902a. *Grab- und Denksteine des Mittleren Reichs im Museum von Kairo II (No. 20400–20780)* (Reichsdruckerei: Berlin).

1902b. *Grab- und Denksteine des Mittleren Reichs im Museum von Kairo IV (No. 20001–20780)* (Reichsdruckerei: Berlin).

Leahy, Anthony. 1989. 'A protective measure at Abydos in the Thirteenth Dynasty', *Journal of Egyptian Archaeology* 75: 41–60.

Levenson, Felix. 2019. 'Monuments and monumentality – different perspectives', in Federico Buccellati, Sebastian Hageneuer, Sylva van der Heyden, and Felix Levenson (eds.), *Size matters: Understanding monumentality across Ancient Civilizations* (transcript Verlag: Bielefeld), 17–39.

Lichtheim, Miriam. 1992. *Maat in Egyptian autobiographies and related studies* (Universitätsverlag: Freiburg).

Luiselli, Maria Michela. 2011. 'The ancient Egyptian scene of "Pharaoh simiting his enemies": An attempt to visualize cultural memory?' in Martin Bommas (ed.), *Cultural memory and identity in ancient societies* (Continuum: London), 10–25.

Ma, John. 2007. 'Hellenistic honorific statues and their inscriptions', in Zahra Newby and Ruth Leader-Newby (eds.), *Art and inscription in the ancient world* (Cambridge University Press: Cambridge), 203–20.

McAnany, Patricia A. 1995. *Living with the ancestors: Kinship and kingship in ancient Maya society* (University of Texas Press: Austin).

Meskell, Lynn. 2003. 'Memory's materiality: Ancestral presence, commemorative practice and disjunctive locales', in Ruth M. Van Dyke and Susan E. Alcock (eds.), *Archaeologies of memory* (Blackwell: Malden, MA), 34–55.

2004. *Object worlds in ancient Egypt: Material biographies past and present* (Berg: Oxford).

2007. 'Back to the future: From the past in the present to the past in the past', in Norman Yoffee (ed.), *Negotiating the past in the past: Identity, memory, and landscape in archaeological research* (University of Arizona Press: Tucson), 215–26.

Millard, Anne. 1976. 'The Position of Women in the Family and in Society in Ancient Egypt, with Special Reference to the Middle Kingdom', PhD, UCL.

Miller, Daniel. 2005. 'Materiality: An introduction', in Daniel Miller (ed.), *Materiality* (Duke University Press: Durham, NC), 1–50.

Mixter, David W. 2017. 'Collective remembering in archaeology: A relational approach to ancient Maya memory', *Journal of Archaeological Method and Theory* 24: 261–302.

Mohr, Herta Therese. 1943. *The mastaba of Hetep-her-akhti: Study on an Egyptian tomb chapel in the Museum of Antiquities, Leiden* (E. J. Brill: Leiden).

Morris, Ellen. 2023. *Famine and feast in ancient Egypt* (Cambridge University Press: Cambridge).

Morris, Ellen F. 2020. 'Writing trauma: Ipuwer and the curation of cultural memory', in Richard E. Averbeck and K. Lawson Younger (eds.), *'An excellent fortress for his armies, a refuge for the people': Egyptological, archaeological, and biblical studies in honor of James K. Hoffmeier* (Eisenbrauns: University Park, TX), 231–52.

Myers, Adrian T. 2008. 'Between memory and materiality: An archaeological approach to studying the Nazi Concentration Camps', *Journal of Conflict Archaeology* 4: 231–45.

Navrátilová, Hana. 2020. 'Visitors' graffiti: Traces of a re-appropriation of sacred spaces and a demonstration of literacy in the landscape', in Miroslav Bárta and Jiří Janák (eds.), *Profane landscapes, sacred spaces: Urban development in the Bronze Age southern Levant* (Equinox: Sheffield), 141–57.

Nelson-Hurst, Melinda G. 2010. '" ... who causes his name to live": The vivification formula through the Second Intermediate Period', in

Zahi Hawass and Jennifer Houser Wegner (eds.), *Millions of jubilees: Studies in honor of David P. Silverman* (Conseil Suprême des Antiquités de l'Égypte: Cairo), 13–31.

Nora, Pierre. 1989. 'Between memory and history: les lieux de mémoire', *Representations* 26: 7–24.

O'Connor, David. 1967. 'Abydos: A preliminary report of the Pennsylvania-Yale Expedition, 1967', *Expedition* 10: 10–23.

  1985. 'The "cenotaphs" of the Middle Kingdom at Abydos', in Paule Posener-Kriéger (ed.), *Mélanges Gamal Eddin Mokhtar II* (Institut français d'archéologie orientale du Caire: Cairo), 161–77.

  2009. *Abydos: Egypt's first pharaohs and the cult of Osiris* (Thames & Hudson: London).

Olabarria, Leire. 2012. 'El hermano de la madre y el hijo de la hermana en el Reino Medio', in Luís Manuel De Araújo and José das Candeias Sales (eds.), *Novos trabalhos de egiptologia ibérica. IV congresso ibérico de egiptologia. IV congreso ibérico de egiptología* (Instituto Oriental e Centro de História da Facultade de Letras da Universidade de Lisboa: Lisbon), 878–98.

  2018. 'Formulating relations: An approach to the smyt-formula', *Zeitschrift für Ägyptische Sprache und Altertumskunde* 145: 57–70.

  2020a. 'Coming to terms with stelae: A performative approach to memorial stelae and chapels of Abydos in the Middle Kingdom', *Studien zur altägyptischen Kultur* 49: 117–77.

  2020b. *Kinship and family in ancient Egypt: Archaeology and anthropology in dialogue* (Cambridge University Press: Cambridge).

  forthcoming. 'Monumental lives: The chapel of Ikhernofret as a distributed biography', Peeters: Leuven.

Olick, Jeffrey K. 2023. 'The future of the Mnemonic Turn', *Social Research: An International Quarterly* 90: 781–807.

Olick, Jeffrey K., Vered Vinitzky-Seroussi, and Daniel Levy (eds.). 2011. *The collective memory reader* (Oxford University Press: New York).

Olivier, Laurent. 2004. 'The past of the present: Archaeological memory and time', *Archaeological Dialogues* 10: 204–13.

Oppenheim, Adela, Dorothea Arnold, Dieter Arnold, and Kei Yamamoto. 2015. *Ancient Egypt transformed: The Middle Kingdom* (Yale University Press: New Haven, CT).

Osborne, James F. 2014. 'Monuments and monumentality', in James F. Osborne (ed.), *Approaching monumentality in archaeology* (State University of New York Press: Albany), 1–19.

2017. 'Counter-monumentality and the vulnerability of memory', *Journal of Social Archaeology* 17: 163–87.

Osorio G. Silva, Luiza. 2023. 'Out of ruins: Contextualizing an ancient Egyptian Spectacle of architectural reuse', *Cambridge Archaeological Journal* 33: 521–36.

Parkinson, Richard B. 2020. 'The sensory worlds of ancient Egypt', in Robin Skeates and Jo Day (eds.), *The Routledge handbook of sensory archaeology* (Routledge: Abingdon), 413–33.

Petrie, W. M. Flinders. 1901. *The royal tombs of the earliest dynasties: 1901, Part 2* (Egypt Exploration Fund: London).

1903. *Abydos. Part II. 1903* (Egypt Exploration Society: London).

1916. 'A cemetery portal', *Ancient Egypt* 4: 174–80.

Petts, David. 2003. 'Memories in stone: Changing strategies and contexts of remembrance in early medieval Wales', in Howard Williams (ed.), *Archaeologies of remembrance: Death and memory in past societies* (Kluwer Academic/Plenum: New York), 193–213.

Quirke, Stephen. 2003. '"Art" and "the artist" in late Middle Kingdom administration', in Stephen Quirke (ed.), *Discovering Egypt from the Neva: The Egyptological legacy of Oleg D. Berlev* (Achet: Berlin), 85–105.

2004. *Titles and bureaux of Egypt 1850–1700 BC* (Golden House: London).

Ragazzoli, Chloé C. D. 2013. 'The social creation of a scribal place: The visitors' inscriptions in the tomb attributed to Antefiqer (TT 60)', *Studien zur altägyptischen Kultur* 42: 269–323.

Ramond, Pierre. 1977. *Les stèles égyptiennes du Musée G. Labit à Toulouse* (Institut français d'archeologie orientale: Cairo).

Regulski, Ilona. 2014. 'The origins and early development of writing in Egypt', in *The Oxford Handbook of Topics in Archaeology* (Oxford Academic: online edition). https://doi.org/10.1093/oxfordhb/9780199935413.013.61.

Richards, Janet E. 1999. 'Conceptual landscapes in the Egyptian Nile Valley', in Wendy Ashmore and A. Bernard Knapp (eds.), *Archaeologies of landscape: Contemporary perspectives* (Blackwell: Oxford), 83–100.

2005. *Society and death in ancient Egypt: Mortuary landscapes of the Middle Kingdom* (Cambridge University Press: Cambridge).

Rizzo, Jérôme. 2024. *Perpétuer le nom (sanx rn): une liturgie mémorielle dans l'ancienne Égypte* (Equipe Egypte Nilotique et Méditerranéenne: Montpellier).

Rodríguez-Berzosa Gómez-Landero, Sara. 2016. 'La lactancia en el antiguo Egipto', PhD, Universitat Autònoma de Barcelona.

Rohl, Darrell J. 2015. 'Place theory, genealogy, and the cultural biography of Roman monuments', in Tom Brindle, Martyn Allen, Emma Durham, and

Alex Smith (eds.), *TRAC 2014: Proceedings of the twenty-fourth annual theoretical Roman archaeology conference, Reading 2014* (Oxbow Books: Oxford), 1–16.

Rosenfeld, Gavriel D. 2009. 'A looming crash or a soft landing? Forecasting the future of the memory "industry"', *The Journal of Modern History* 81: 122–58.

Röttger-Rössler, Birgitt. 1993. 'Autobiography in question: On self presentation and life description in an Indonesian Society', *Anthropos* 88: 365–73.

Schacter, Daniel L. 2001. *Forgotten ideas, neglected pioneers: Richard Semon and the story of memory* (Psycholoby Press: Philadelphia, PA).

Shubert, Steven Blake. 2007. 'Those who (still) live on earth: A study of the ancient Egyptian appeal to the living texts', PhD, University of Toronto.

Silverman, David P. 1989. 'The so-called Portal Temple of Ramesses II at Abydos', in Sylvia Schoske (ed.), *Akten des vierten Internationalen Ägyptologen Kon gresses München 1985. Band 2: Archäologie, Feldforschung, Prähistorie* (Buske: Hamburg), 269–77.

Simpson, William Kelly. 1974. *The terrace of the great god at Abydos: The offering chapels of dynasties 12 and 13* (Peabody Museum of Natural History of Yale University; University Museum of the University of Pennsylvania: New Haven, CT; Philadelphia, PA).

1995. *Inscribed material from the Pennsylvania-Yale excavations at Abydos* (Peabody Museum of Natural History of Yale University; University of Pennsylvania Museum of Archaeology and Anthropology: New Haven, CT; Philadelphia, PA).

(ed.). 2003. *The literature of ancient Egypt: An anthology of stories, instructions, stelae, autobiographies, and poetry* (Yale University Press: New Haven, CT).

Smith, Mark. 2017. *Following Osiris: Perspectives on the Osirian afterlife from four millennia* (Oxford University Press: Oxford).

Snape, Steven. 2011. *Ancient Egyptian tombs: The cultures of life and death* (Wiley-Blackwell: Malden).

2019. 'Memorial monuments at Abydos and the "Terrace of the Great God"', in Ilona Regulski (ed.), *Abydos: The sacred land at the western horizon* (Peeters: Leuven), 255–72.

Spiegelberg, Wilhelm. 1908. 'Eine Formel der Grabsteine', *Zeitschrift für Ägyptische Sprache und Altertumskunde* 45: 67–71.

Stauder-Porchet, Julie. 2017. *Les autobiographies de l'Ancien Empire égyptien: étude sur la naissance d'un genre* (Peeters: Leuven).

2020. 'Genres and textual prehistories of the Egyptian autobiography in the old kingdom', in Julie Stauder-Porchet, Elizabeth Frood and Andréas Stauder (eds.), *Ancient Egyptian biographies: contexts, forms, functions* (Lockwood: Atlanta), 87–116.

Stefanović, Danijela. 2005. 'The holders of the title iry pDt in the period of the Middle Kingdom: prosopography', *Journal of Egyptological Studies* 2: 75–88.

2006. *The holders of regular military titles in the period of the Middle Kingdom: Dossiers* (Golden House: London).

2008a. 'The non-royal women of the Middle Kingdom I – mnat', *Göttinger Miszellen* 216: 79–90.

2008b. 'šmsw: Soldiers of the Middle Kingdom', *Wiener Zeitschrift für die Kunde des Morgenlandes* 98: 233–48.

2010. 'The stela of wr-nTr at Saffron Walden Museum', *Chronique d'Égypte* 85: 41–50.

2012. 'sš qdwt: The attestations from the Middle Kingdom and the Second Intermediate Period', in Katalin Anna Kóthay (ed.), *Art and Society. Ancient and Modern Contexts of Egyptian Art. Proceedings of the International Conference held at the Museum of Fine Arts, Budapest, 13–15 May 2010* (Museum of Fine Arts: Budapest), 185–98.

Strauss, Jean A. 2018. 'Les contrats et les reçus de salaire de nourrice relatifs à des esclaves dans la documentation papyrologique grecque de l'Égypte romaine', *Papyrologica Lupiensia* 27: 69–95.

Sullivan, Elaine A. 2020. *Constructing the sacred: Visibility and ritual landscape at the Egyptian necropolis of Saqqara* (Stanford University Press: Palo Alto).

Taylor, John H. 2019. 'Objects from Abydos in early 19th-century British collections: Rediscovering "lost" provenance and context', in Ilona Regulski (ed.), *Abydos: The sacred land at the western horizon* (Peeters: Leuven), 273–300.

Taylor, Timothy. 2009. 'Materiality', in R. Alexander Bentley, Herbert D. G. Maschner and Christopher Chippindale (eds.), *Handbook of archaeological theories* (Alta Mira Press: Lanham), 297–320.

Thomas, Julian S. 2007. 'The trouble with material culture', *Journal of Iberian Archaeology* 9/10: 11–24.

Tilley, Christopher. 1994. *A phenomenology of landscape: Places, paths and monuments* (Berg: Oxford; Providence).

Troche, Julia. 2021. *Death, power, and apotheosis in ancient Egypt: The Old and Middle Kingdoms* (Cornell University Press: Ithaca).

Truc, Gérôme. 2011. 'Memory of places and places of memory: For a Halbwachsian socio-ethonography of collective memory', *International Social Science Journal* 203–4: 147–59.

Tulving, Endel. 1972. 'Episodic and semantic memory', in Endel Tulving, Wayne Donaldson and Gordon H. Bower (eds.), *Organization of memory* (Academic Press: New York), 381–403.

Van Dyke, Ruth M. 2009. 'Chaco reloaded: Discursive social memory on the post-Chacoan landscape', *Journal of Social Archaeology* 9: 220–48.

2019. 'Archaeology and social memory', *Annual Review of Anthropology* 48: 207–25.

Van Dyke, Ruth M., and Susan E. Alcock (eds.). 2003a. *Archaeologies of memory* (Blackwell: Malden, MA).

2003b. 'Archaeologies of memory: An introduction', in Ruth M. Van Dyke and Susan E. Alcock (eds.), *Archaeologies of memory* (Blackwell: Malden, MA), 1–13.

Végh, Zsuzsanna. 2019. 'The mᶜḥᶜ.t of Osiris in Asyut', in Ilona Regulski (ed.), *Abydos: The sacred land at the western horizon* (Peeters: Leuven), 301–13.

2021. *Feste der Ewigkeit: Untersuchungen zu den abydenischen Kulten während des Alten und Mittleren Reiches* (Mohr Siebeck: Tübingen).

Vernus, Pascal. 1973. 'Un fragment du Moyen Empire', *Revue d'Égyptologie* 25: 255–56.

1976. 'La formule "le souffle de la bouche" au Moyen Empire', *Revue d'Égyptologie* 28: 139–45.

Vinitzky-Seroussi, Vered. 2001. 'Review of "Memory and methodology" by Susannah Radstone (2000)', *American Ethnologist* 28: 494–6.

Weiss, Lara 2022. *The walking dead at Saqqara: Strategies of social and religious interaction in practice.* Religionsgeschichtliche Versuche und Vorarbeiten 78 (De Gruyter: Berlin).

Wendrich, Willeke. 2010. 'Egyptian archaeology: from text to context', in Willeke Wendrich (ed.), *Egyptian Archaeology* (Wiley-Blackwell: Oxford), 1–14.

Whelan, Paul. 2016. 'On the context and conception of two "trademark" styles from late Middle Kingdom Abydos,' in Gianluca Miniaci and Wolfram Grajetzki (eds.), *The world of Middle Kingdom Egypt (2000– 1550 BC): Contributions on archaeology, art, religion, and written sources* (Golden House Publications: London), 285–338.

Williams, Howard (ed.). 2003a. *Archaeologies of remembrance: Death and memory in past societies* (Kluwer Academic/Plenum: New York).

2003b. 'Introduction: The archaeology of death, memory, and material culture,' in Howard Williams (ed.), *Archaeologies of remembrance: Death and memory in past societies* (Kluwer Academic/Plenum: New York), 1–24.

Yamamoto, Kei. 2009. 'A Middle Kingdom pottery assemblage from North Abydos', PhD, University of Toronto.

2015. 'The art of the stela: An appeal to the living,' in Adela Oppenheim, Dorothea Arnold, Dieter Arnold and Kei Yamamoto (eds.), *Ancient Egypt transformed: The Middle Kingdom* (Yale University Press: New Haven), 33–6.

Zinn, Katharina. 2018. 'Literacy in pharaonic Egypt: Orality and literacy between agency and memory', in Anne Kolb (ed.), *Literacy in ancient everyday life* (De Gruyter: Berlin), 67–97.

Acknowledgements

This Element is the result of several years of work. I started thinking about memory and commemoration during my DPhil at the University of Oxford, when I was curious about the effect monumental display would have had on conceptualisations of social groups and dissemination of social knowledge in Middle Kingdom Egypt. Since then, I have become less inclined to focus on transmission, and more interested in assemblage thinking instead. The emergence of memory within networks of interactions between human and non-human agents is the kernel of the approach advocated in this Element.

The ideas that I explore arise from diverse readings as well as from discussions with various colleagues over the years. I am grateful to my colleagues at the University of Birmingham for providing a convivial space to think about ancient cultures from a cross-disciplinary perspective. I am fortunate to have exceptional doctoral students, Cannon Fairbairn, Reuben Hutchinson-Wong, Liv Kirk, Sam Powell, and Valentina Santini; our conversations have fuelled me to think and write about memory in new and creative ways. I have given lectures on memory in Oxford, Liverpool, Birmingham, Cambridge, and Turin. I want to thank all the attendees for their comments and feedback, which have helped me shape my thoughts and strengthen the arguments that I present in this volume. I also led a two-day workshop on materiality in Madrid that allowed me to test some of the ideas developed in Section 3 with an engaging and sympathetic audience. My work on reception, particularly together with my colleague Dr Ellie Dobson, has been invaluable in allowing me to think more widely about the implications of the past in the present after many years focusing on the past in the past.

I am grateful to the editors for their kind invitation to write this Element and for their patience with delays in the submission of the manuscript. I also want to extend my thanks to the two anonymous peer reviewers for their generous and encouraging feedback, which has given me food for thought and helped me nuance some of the ideas presented here.

Finally, I would like to dedicate this Finite Element to my partner Iñaki, proof-reader extraordinaire and unmatched Egyptological consort. Here is to many more years of making memories together.

Cambridge Elements ☰

Ancient Egypt in Context

Gianluca Miniaci

University of Pisa

Gianluca Miniaci is Associate Professor in Egyptology at the University of Pisa, Honorary
Researcher at the Institute of Archaeology, UCL – London, and Chercheur associé
at the École Pratique des Hautes Études, Paris. He is currently co-director of the
archaeological mission at Zawyet Sultan (Menya, Egypt). His main research interest focuses
on the social history and the dynamics of material culture in Middle Bronze Age
Egypt and its interconnections between the Levant, Aegean, and Nubia.

Juan Carlos Moreno García

CNRS, Paris

Juan Carlos Moreno García (PhD in Egyptology, 1995) is a CNRS senior researcher at the
Sorbonne University, as well as lecturer on social and economic history of ancient Egypt at
the École des Hautes Études en Sciences Sociales (EHESS) in Paris. He has published
extensively on the administration, socio-economic history, and landscape organization of
ancient Egypt, usually in a comparative perspective with other civilizations of the ancient
world, and has organized several conferences on these topics.

Anna Stevens

University of Cambridge and Monash University

Anna Stevens is a research archaeologist with a particular interest in how material
culture and urban space can shed light on the lives of the non-elite in ancient Egypt. She is
Senior Research Associate at the McDonald Institute for Archaeological Research and
Assistant Director of the Amarna Project (both University of Cambridge).

About the Series

The aim of this Elements series is to offer authoritative but accessible overviews of
foundational and emerging topics in the study of ancient Egypt, along with
comparative analyses, translated into a language comprehensible to non-specialists.
Its authors will take a step back and connect ancient Egypt to the world around,
bringing ancient Egypt to the attention of the broader humanities community and
leading Egyptology in new directions.

Cambridge Elements ≡

Ancient Egypt in Context

Elements in the Series

Printed in the United States
by Baker & Taylor Publisher Services